THE SEVEN SPIRITS

OR

WHAT I TEACH MY OFFICERS

THE SEVEN SPIRITS

OR

WHAT I TEACH MY OFFICERS

BY

GENERAL WILLIAM BOOTH

THE SALVATION ARMY SUPPLIES and
PURCHASING DEPARTMENT
Atlanta, Georgia

First Printing – 1985

Printed in the U.S.A.

Original edition printed - 1907
Campfield Press
St. Albans, England

Available through book stores
or Salvation Army Supplies

Published by
The Salvation Army
Supplies and Purchasing Department
1424 Northeast Expressway
Atlanta, Georgia U.S.A. 30329

FOREWORD

Thank God for the printed page, by which we are able to catch once again the flaming spirit of the Founder.

That will surely be the experience of all readers of this reprint edition of a series of addresses by General William Booth delivered to Salvation Army officers at the 1904 International Congress in London.

Here is an authentic reproduction of written notes from which the Founder spoke on the sub-topic, *What I Teach My Officers.*

Both timely and timeless, the General's writings continue to have a revivifying influence upon officers in this day and age. We pray that this volume will provide refreshing reading as we rededicate our-selves to the high and holy principles so strongly stated by the Founder. God bless The Salvation Army!

Atlanta, Georgia
May 4, 1985

Commissioner Andrew S. Miller
Territorial Commander

PREFATORY NOTE

This volume contains the outlines of a series of addresses by General William Booth, delivered to Salvation Army officers at the International Congress held in London, in June, 1904.

That which is here printed does not profess to be a verbatim report of those addresses but is merely a reproduction of the written notes from which General Booth spoke, and is issued in this form in reply to an oft-repeated request for information as to the teaching given by the General to his officers.

INTERNATIONAL HEADQUARTERS,

May, 1907

THE SEVEN SPIRITS

CHAPTER I

INTRODUCTORY

SECTION I

I. *A great opportunity lies before The Army, and before you as representatives of The Army.*

You have looked at that opportunity; you have wondered about it, and, if you are men and women of God, which I believe you are, your souls are stirred with gratitude at the thought that God has honoured you by any association with a movement that has been the means of so greatly glorifying Him, and so largely blessing the world.

II. *The use that is made of this mighty opportunity for promoting the happiness of mankind, and the glory of the God of Heaven, very largely depends upon the Field Officers of The Salvation Army.*

Officers make the character of the armies they lead.

This is true of military armies—Napoleon not only led his army, but made it.

This is true of commercial armies. The great financiers and traders mould the business world.

The same may be said of political armies.

This is equally true, if not more so, of Salvation Armies. On you, then, this responsibility rests.

The Field Officer especially fashions the force he controls, chiefly in three ways: by his mind, character, and methods. In short, he constitutes the mould in which those whom he commands will be cast.

The shape you give the men and women under your command to-day will go down to the third, the fourth, and the fifth generations. You are making the kind of Salvationists who will be walking about here five hundred years hence, if the world lasts so long.

If the Officer is a coward, those whom he commands will be cowards. If he is holy, they will be holy. If he is a man of resistless courage and daring, they will be like him.

Our responsibility for success or failure is therefore enormous. Where we are successful we are not only gaining victories to-day, but making the conquerors of the future.

Let us remember—we shall have to give an account of our stewardship; we are passing over, one by one, to that great Tribunal. My dear wife, Commissioner Dowdle, the Consul, have all gone to give their account. We too shall have to go. The words, "Behold I come quickly," are ever sounding in my ears.

III. *What kind of Officers are required to meet this opportunity?*

I think I possess some ability for pointing out the qualities needed for satisfactorily answering this question.

1. I have read my Bible and pondered over the great responsibilities which lie at the very foundation of an Officer's duties. I hope I have not read that Book in vain.

2. I have listened to the voice of the Spirit of God within me. He has shown me something of what an Officer should be and do, in order that he may efficiently fulfil the mission to which he has been called.

3. I have studied the hearts and circumstances of the men you are sent to save. Human nature is, as we very often say, much the same in all ages and in all places.

    What I have seen of the failings, the prejudices, and the sins of men with regard to religion during my life should be of service in helping and guiding you in your warfare.

4. I have profited by the experience of other warriors on the field: from those of the prophets down to the last Army Captain who has any reputation for bringing men to God.

    In the days of old, men walked over land, and sailed over water, thousands of miles, penetrating the depths of barren wildernesses and tractless forests, in order to gaze upon some skeleton hermit who had acquired a special reputation for holiness, or who had gained a more intimate knowledge than his fellows of the dealings of God with men.

    Something like this has been my custom ever since I was a youth, fifteen years of age. To hear of anyone possessing any extra skill in soul-saving has been enough to excite my curiosity, lead me to seek a knowledge of their doings, and carry me to their feet.

Surely, I must have learned something from these worthies. What I have learned I want to tell you.

5. I have studied the needs of the world around me.

A large part of my life has been spent in considering and mourning over the sins and sorrows of men, and in making plans for their deliverance.

6. I have had some personal experience in this warfare.

It is nearly sixty years now since I made my first attempt to influence men in favour of salvation.

Could I tell the number of individuals whom during that time I have seen kneeling at the mercy-seat it would sound like a fiction.

Perhaps I have been as highly privileged in this respect as any man that ever lived. God has indeed endorsed my work with His blessing.

I think I know you, my comrades, and have some idea of what you are able to do, and the circumstances in which you are called to labour, and I am sure my heart will not allow me to ask from you what is beyond your ability to give. Nothing can be gained by seeking impossibilities.

SECTION II

I. *I propose to tell you frankly what I think is the kind of Officer called for at this juncture of our history ; and, among other things, I think he should answer to the following description :—*

1. *He should be possessed of the Spirit of Divine Life.* Dead things will be of no use here.
2. *He should be possessed of the Spirit of Holiness.* Sanctified men are the world's great need.

3. *He should be possessed of the Spirit of Supreme Devotion to the Object of The Army.*
Given up without any secret reservations.
4. *He should be possessed of the Spirit of Light.*
Making men know themselves, and know the things of God.
5. *He should be possessed of the Spirit of War.*
With fighting Officers The Army can conquer the world.
6. *He should be possessed of the Spirit of Faith.*
" All things are possible to him that believeth."
7. *He should be possessed of the Spirit of Burning Love.*
Love never faileth. Love shall be the conqueror.

II. *You may take the possession of these qualifications as being the will of God concerning every one of you.*

You may take them as commandments coming directly from God Himself.

In the book of Revelation John speaks of the Seven Spirits of God which are before His Throne, and which go out into all the earth to make men know what is the mind of God respecting them.

These Seven Spirits are still travelling to and fro on their heavenly mission. These Seven Spirits have voices, and speak to the consciences of men. They wait to speak to us. They proclaim what is their Master's will concerning the Officers of The Salvation Army. They will come to dwell with us, and help us to carry out the object for which we exist.

Shall we hear them? Shall we receive them? What do you say? I know your mind. I answer for you. Yes, certainly we will. Let us welcome them as the messengers of God. This they most certainly are.

SECTION III

I. *Here they come. The first Spirit enters. Look at him. Oh, vision of beauty! How can I paint him?*

More beautiful in appearance, but in appearance only, than those who follow him. Lovely roses on his cheeks; quick, vigorous, and active his every movement, while his eyes flash every moment with lustrous light and living fire. In his hand he holds a banner. On one side it bears a representation of the morning sun, and on the other a white-robed spirit rising from the tomb. *This is the Spirit of Life.*

He speaks. Listen! He says: " O Officers, Officers, I am one of the Seven Spirits whom John saw. I travel up and down the earth on special errands of mercy. I am come from Him that sitteth on the Throne, and reigneth for ever and ever, to tell you that if you are to succeed in your life-and-death struggle for God and man, the first thing you must possess, in all its full and rich maturity, is *the Spirit of Divine Life.*"

II. *And now here is the second Spirit.*

Beautiful again, beautiful beyond human conception or description; benign of countenance, and calm and restful in manner, with gentle and heart-moving speech; clothed in white and spotless raiment; holy and undefiled. *This is the Spirit of Purity.*

But see, he spreads forth his wings and looks down upon us and speaks. Hear him : " O Officers, Officers, the Great Father has sent me to tell you that if you would be successful in your campaign against wickedness, selfishness, and fiends, *you must yourselves be holy.*"

III. *Now enters the third Spirit.*

Look at him. He is of an even more imposing
appearance than those who have preceded him.
Upon his shoulders is inscribed a crimson cross;
round his loins is a girdle of blood-stained raiment.
His bosom heaves with anguish on account of the
oppressions, sins, and miseries of a suffering world.
This is the Spirit of Devotion.

Hear him. He speaks : " O Officers, Officers, you
must be supremely given up to the saving of men."

IV. *And now here comes the fourth Spirit.*

Look at him. He has a strong, determined countenance,
and there is a fiery Cross upon his breast. In his
right hand he holds a flaming sword, and in his left a
summons to the Judgment Bar. *This is the Spirit of
War.*

Now he speaks. Hear him : " O Officers, Officers, you
must fight devils, lies, fleshly indulgences, hardships,
disappointments, and everything that sets itself up
against God, or that is opposed to the living of a holy
life, or which threatens the damnation of men. O
Officers, at all risks and consequences you must fight
for God and the salvation of souls."

V. *Now enters the fifth Spirit.*

Here he comes, bright as the sun at noonday, with
eyes before and behind, while shafts of living light
go forth from his brow at every turn. See, he holds
the Word of God in one hand, and the Morning Star
in the other. *This is the Spirit of Truth.*

Hear him. He speaks : " O Officers, Officers, your
work is to make men know the unchanging and the

unchangeable truth about the Love of God, the efficacy of the Blood of the Lamb, the accursedness of evil, the cruelty of the devil, the terrors of the Great White Throne, the joys of Heaven, and the horrors of the damnation of Hell. To do this you must be filled with the Light yourselves."

VI. *Now for the sixth Spirit.*

Behold him—with eyes lifted up to Heaven and stedfastly fixed on the Throne of God; with bold, unshrinking confidence stamped on every feature. In his hand he holds a crimson banner, on which there is inscribed in letters of gold: "I believe." *This is the Spirit of Faith.*

He speaks. Hear him: "O Officers, Officers, you cannot do without me. Listen to my words. If you treasure them up in your hearts, and carry them out in your lives, you shall be conquerors. If you neglect them, you will be defeated, no matter how brave you are in other things. You must take the inscription on my banner as your life-long motto. You must believe. You must do it night and day, in sorrow and joy, in defeat and in victory, living and dying. You must be men and women of Faith."

VII. *But here comes the most beautiful and entrancing Spirit of all.*

Who can describe her? No one, for she is divine. Her countenance beams with holy affection, and speaks of inward rapture, and yet her eyes are full of compassionate tears. She is enveloped in a celestial flame, the emblem of the fire that is burning in her breast, while her arms are extended as though they

would enfold the whole sinning, sorrowing world in
their embrace. Oh, loveliest of all God's creations,
who art thou? *This is the Spirit of Burning Love.*
Hear her. She speaks: "O Officers, Officers; commissioned by the great 'I Am,' I come to tell you
that in all you think, or speak, or do love must be
the ruling passion of your lives. You must love each
other. You must love your Soldiers. You must love
poor sinners. You must love God; and that not after
a fickle, cold, half-hearted fashion, but with a changeless, quenchless, burning love."

What shall we say to these Spirits? What reply shall
they carry back to the Throne? What answer shall
we give to the appeals they make to us in our own
hearts? Let us say, "O ye Seven Spirits, we
believe; nay, we feel that you have brought us the
words of God Himself; and those words we will,
more than ever, set ourselves to obey."

And in order that we may do so, my comrades, let us
consider them in the order in which their messages
have been given to us.

CHAPTER II

THE SPIRIT OF LIFE

Section I

We begin with the good Spirit—the Spirit of Life.
What did he say? What were the words he brought
to us from the Throne? Let me repeat them: " O
Officers, Officers, I am one of the Seven Spirits whom
John saw. I travel up and down the earth on special
errands of mercy. I am come from Him that sitteth
on the Throne, and reigneth for ever and ever, to tell
you that if you are going to succeed in your life-and-
death struggle for God and man, the first thing you
must possess, in all its full and rich maturity, is the
Spirit of Divine Life."

I. *Now, before I go to the direct consideration of this
message, let me have a word or two about life
itself.*

Life, as you know, is the opposite principle to death.
To be alive is to possess an inward force capable
of action without any outside assistance. For
instance: anything that has in it the principle by
which it is able to act in some way, independent
of the will of any other thing or creature outside
of itself, may be said to be alive. It has in it
the principle of life.

II. *This principle of life is the mainspring and glory of God's Universe.*

We have it in different forms in this world. For instance :

1. We have material life. There is living and dead water, and there is living and dead earth.

2. Then there is vegetable life. In the fields, and woods, and gardens, you have living trees, and flowers, and seeds.

3. Then there is animal life. Only think of the variety, and usefulness, and instinctive skill of unnumbered members of the animal world.

4. Then, rising higher in the scale of being, you have human life. Every man, woman, and child possesses, as it were, a trinity of existence; namely, physical life, mental life, and soul life; each being a marvel in itself.

5. Then, rising higher still, we have a life more important, and bringing more glory to God than any of the other forms that I have noticed, and that is *Spiritual Life.*

SECTION II

On this Spiritual Life let me make one or two remarks.

I. *Spiritual Life is Divine in its origin.*

It is a creation of the Holy Spirit. I need not dwell on this truth. Jesus Christ was at great trouble to teach it. " Marvel not," He said, " ye must be born again. That which is born of the flesh is flesh, and that which is born of the Spirit is spirit." You have gone through this experience yourselves. You must insist on it in your people. Spiritual life proceeds from God. It can be obtained in no other way.

II. *Spiritual Life not only proceeds from God, but partakes of the Nature of God.*

We see this principle, that the life imparted partakes of the nature of the author of being that imparts it, illustrated around us in every direction.

The tree partakes of the nature of the tree from which it is derived. The animal partakes of the nature of the creature that begets it. The child partakes of the nature of its parents. So the soul, born of God, will possess the nature of its Author. Its life will be divine.

This is a mystery. We cannot understand it, but the Apostle distinctly affirms it when he says, the Son of God is a partaker of the Divine nature.

III. *Spiritual Life, like all other life, carries with it the particular powers belonging to its own nature.*

Every kind of life has its own particular powers—senses, instincts, or whatever they may be called.

1. Vegetable life has its powers, enabling it to draw nutrition out of the ground.

2. Fish life has power adapting it to an existence in the water.

3. Animal life has powers or senses suitable to its sphere of existence, such as : seeing, hearing, tasting, and the like.

4. Human life has—

   (*a*) Faculties, emotions, loves and hatreds, suitable to its manner of existence.

   (*b*) And it has its own peculiar destiny. It goes back to God, to be judged as to its conduct when its earthly career terminates.

(c) And the spiritual life of which we are speaking has powers or faculties necessary to the maintenance of its existence, and to the discharge of the duties appropriate to the sphere in which it moves. For instance: it has powers to draw from God the nourishment it requires; it has powers to see or discern spiritual things; it has powers to distinguish holy people; it has powers to love truth, and to hate falsehood; it has powers to suffer and sacrifice for the good of others. It has powers to know, and love, and glorify its Maker.

IV. *Those possessed of this Spiritual Life, like all other beings, act according to their nature.*

For instance: the tree grows in the woods, and bears leaves and fruit after its own nature. The bird flies in the air, builds its nest, and sings its song after its own nature. The wild beasts roam through the forest, and rage and devour according to their own nature. If you are to make these or any other creatures act differently, you must give them a different nature. By distorting the tree, or training the animal, or clipping the wings of the bird, you may make some trifling and temporary alteration in the condition or conduct of these creatures; but when you have done this, left to themselves, they will soon revert to their original nature.

By way of illustration. A menagerie recently paid a visit to a northern town. Amongst the exhibits was a cage labelled " The Happy Family," containing a lion, a tiger, a wolf, and a lamb. When the keeper was asked confidentially how long a time these animals had lived thus peacefully together, he answered, " About ten months. But," said he, with a twinkle in his eye, " the lamb has to be renewed occasionally."

As with these forms of life, so with men and women and children. The only way to secure conduct of a lasting character different from its nature is by effecting a change in that nature. Make them new creatures in Christ Jesus and you will have a Christlike life.

V. *The presence of the powers natural to Spiritual Life constitutes the only true and sufficient evidence of its possession.*

The absence of these powers shows conclusively the absence of the life. If a man does not love God and walk humbly with Him; if he does not long after holiness, love his comrades, and care for souls, it will be satisfying evidence that he has gone back to the old nature—that is, to spiritual death.

VI. *All Spiritual Life is not only imparted by Jesus Christ, but sustained by direct union with Him.*

" I am the Vine," He says, " ye are the branches; he that abideth in Me, and I in him, the same bringeth forth much fruit ; for without Me ye can do nothing." (*John* xv. 6.)

VII. *Nothing will make up for the lack of this life.*

This, indeed, applies to every kind of existence.

1. You cannot find a substitute for life in the vegetable kingdom. Try the trees in the garden. Look at that dead apple tree. As you see it there, it is useless, ugly, fruitless. What will make up for the absence of life? Will the digging, or the manuring of the ground around it do this? No! That will be all in vain. If it is dead, there is only one remedy, and that is to give it life—new life.

2. Take the animal world.

What can you do to make up for the lack of life in a dog? I read the other day of a lady who had a pet dog. She loved it to distraction. It died. Whatever could she do with it to make up for its loss of life? Well, she might have preserved it, stuffed it, jewelled its eyes, and painted its skin. But had she done so, these things would have been a disappointing substitute. So she buried it, and committed suicide in her grief, and was buried by its side.

3. Take the loss of human life.

What is the use of a dead man? Go to the death-chamber. Look at that corpse. The loved ones are distracted. What can they do? They may dress it, adorn it, appeal to it. But all that human skill and effort can conceive will be in vain. All that the broken hearts can say or do must soon terminate, as did Abraham's mourning for Sarah, when he said, " Give me a piece of land that I may bury my dead out of my sight." Nothing can make up for the lack of life.

4. But this is specially true of the spiritual life of which we are speaking.

(a) Take this in its application to a Corps. If you want an active, generous, fighting, dare-devil Corps, able and willing to drive hell before it, that Corps must be possessed, and that fully, by this spirit of life. Nothing else can effectively take its place. No education, learning, Bible knowledge, theology, social amusements, or anything of the kind will be a satisfactory substitute. The Corps that seeks to put any of these things in the place of life will find them a mockery, a delusion, and a snare; will find them to be only the wraps and trappings of death itself.

(b) And if it is so in the Corps, it is so ten thousand times more in the Officer who commands that Corps—in you!

SECTION III

I. *Spiritual Life is the essential root of every other qualification required by a Salvation Army Officer.*

  1. With it he will be of unspeakable interest.

   (*a*) He will be a pleasure to himself. There is an unspeakable joy in having healthy, exuberant life.

   (*b*) He will be of interest to those about him. Who cares about dead things? Dead flowers—throw them out. Dead animals—eat them. Dead men—bury them. Dead and dying Officers—take them away. Give them another Corps.

   If he is living he will be of interest to all about him. Men with humble abilities, if full of this spiritual life, will be a charm and a blessing wherever they go. Look at the lives and writings of such humble men as Billy Bray, Carvosso, and Hodgson Casson. Their memory is an ointment poured forth to-day after long years have passed away.

  2. Without this life an Officer will be of no manner of use.

   No matter how he may be educated or talented, without life is to be without love; and to be without love, the Apostle tells us, is to be only as "a sounding brass." But it is not that of which I want to speak just now.

II. *Spiritual Life is essential to the preservation of life.*

   The first thing life does for its possessor is to lead him to look after its own protection.

   1. When the principle of life is strong, you will have health and longevity.

   2. When it is weak, you have disease.

   3. When it is extinct, you have decay and rottenness.

III. *Only vigorous Spiritual Life will enable a Salvation Army Officer to effectually discharge the duties connected with his position.*

Life is favourable to activity. It is so with all life. Go into the tropical forests, and see the exuberant growth of everything there. Look at the foliage, the blossom, the fruit. Look at the reptiles crawling at your feet, and take care they do not sting you. Look at the birds chattering and fluttering on the trees, and they will charm you. Look at the animals roving through the woods, and take care they do not devour you.

Contrast all this movement with the empty, barren, silent, Polar regions or the dreary, treeless sands of the African desert.

Go and look at the overflowing, tireless activity of the children. Why are they never still? It is the life that is in them. Go to the man at work. With what glee, and for what a trifling remuneration, he sweats, and lifts and carries the ponderous weights. Go to the soldier in the military war. How he shouts and sings as he marches to deprivations, and wounds, and death.

Even so with spiritual life. It never rests; it never tires; it always sees something great to do, and is always ready to undertake it. What is the explanation? How can we account for it? The answer is, Life—abundant life.

IV. *It is only by the possession of life that The Salvation Army Officer can spread this life.*

That is, reproduce himself, multiply himself, or his kind. This reproduction or multiplication of itself is a characteristic of all life.

1. Take the vegetable kingdom. Every living plant has life-producing seed, or some method of reproducing

itself. The thistle: who can count the number of plants that one thistle can produce in a year? One hundred strawberry plants can be made in ten years to produce more than a thousand million other strawberry plants!

2. Take the animal kingdom. Here each living creature has this reproductive power. They say that a pair of sparrows would in ten years, if all their progeny could be preserved, produce as many birds as there are people on the earth—that is, 1,500,000,000. "Ye are of more value than many sparrows."

3. Just so, this spiritual life is intended to spread itself through the world.

It is to this end it is given to you. God's command to Adam was, " Be fruitful, and multiply, and replenish the earth." How much more does this command apply to you and to me! You are to be progenitors of a world of men and women possessed of spiritual life; the parents of a race of angels. How this is to be done is another question. About that I shall have something to say as we go along. For the moment, I am simply occupied with the fact that you have to call this world of holy beings into existence by spreading this life.

Every Officer here is located in a world of death. Sometimes we style it a dying world, and so it is on its human side, but on its spiritual side it is past dying; it is dead. By that I do not mean that the spiritual nature, that is the soul, ever ceases to be in any man. That will never come to pass. Perhaps nothing once created will ever cease to be. Anyway, man is immortal. The soul can never die. Neither do I mean that there is no spiritual life.

4. By spiritual death we mean that the soul is—

(*a*) Separated from God; no union with Him. In a blind man the organ may be perfect, but not connected.

(*b*) Inactive.

No love for the things God loves. No hatred for the things He hates. Dead to His interests, His kingdom; dead to Him.

(*c*) Corrupt, bad, devilish, etc.

What a valley of dry bones the world appears to the man whose eyes have been opened to see the truth of things. Verily, verily, it is one great cemetery crowded with men, women, and children dead in trespasses and sin. Look for a moment at this graveyard, in which the men around you may be said to lie with their hearts all dead and cold to Christ, and all that concerns their Salvation. Look at it. The men and women and children in your town are buried there. The men and women in your city, in your street. Nay, the very people who come to your Hall to hear you talk on a Sunday night are there. There they lie. Let us read the inscriptions on some of their tombs.

(i.) *Here lies Tom Jones.*

He had a beautiful nature, and a young virtuous wife, and some beautiful children. All starved and wretched through their father's selfish ways. He can't help himself. He says so. He has proved it. He is dead in drunkenness.

(ii.) *Here lies Harry Please-Yourself.*

Mad on footballing, theatres, music halls, dances, and the like. Nothing else morning, noon, or night seems to interest him. There he is, dead in pleasure.

(iii.) *Here lies James Haughtiness.*

Full of high notions about his abilities, or his knowledge, or his family, or his house, or his fortune, or his business, or his dogs, or something. There he is, dead in pride.

(iv.) *Here lies Jane Featherhead.*

Absorbed in her hats, and gowns, and ribbons, and companions, and attainments. There she is, dead in vanity.

(v.) *Here lies Miser Graspall.*

Taken up with his money—sovereigns, dollars, francs, kroner, much or little. " Let me have more and more " is his dream, and his cry, and his aim, by night and day. There he is, dead in covetousness.

(vi.) *Here lies Sceptical Doubtall.*

Hunting through the world of nature, and revolution, and providence, and specially through the dirty world of his own dark little heart, for arguments against God and Christ and Heaven. There he is, dead in infidelity.

(vii.) *Here lies Jeremiah Make-Believe.*

With his Bible Class and Singing Choir, and Sunday religion, and heartless indifference to the Salvation or damnation of the perishing crowds at his door. There he is, dead in formality.

(viii.) *Here lies Surly Badblood.*

Packed full of suspicions and utter disregards for the happiness and feelings of his wife, family, neighbours, or friends. There he is, dead in bad tempers.

(ix.) *Here lies Dives Enjoy-Yourself.*

Look at his marble tomb, and golden coffin, and embroidered shroud, and ermine robes. This is a man whose every earthly want is supplied—Carriages, music, friends. There he is, dead in luxury.

(x.) *Here lies Dick Never-Fear.*

His mouth is filled with laughter, and his heart with contempt when you speak to him about his soul. He has no anxiety, not he. He'll come off all right, never fear. Is not God merciful? And did not Christ die? And did not his mother pray? Don't be alarmed, God won't hurt him. There he is, dead in presumption.

(xi.) *Here lies Judas Renegade.*

His grave has a desolate look. The thorns and thistles grow over it. The occupant has money and worldly friends, and many other things, but altogether he gets no satisfaction out of them; he is uneasy all the time. There he is, dead in apostacy.

There are any number of other graves. It is interesting, although painful, to wander amongst them. All, or nearly all, their occupants are held down by a heavy weight of ignorance, a sense of utter helplessness. And all are bound hand and foot with chains of lust, or passion, or procrastination, of their own forging. In the midst of these graves you live, and move, and have your being.

What is your duty here? Oh, that you realised your true business in this region of death! Having eyes, oh! that you could see. Having ears, oh! that you could hear. Having hearts, oh! that you could feel. What are you going to do with this graveyard? Walk about it in heartless unconcern, or with no higher feeling than gratitude for having been made alive yourselves? Or will you content yourselves with strolling through it, taxing its poor occupants for your living while leaving them quietly in their tombs as hopeless as you found them? Heaven forbid! Well, then, what do you propose? What will you do?

Look after their bodies, and feed and nourish them,
making the graveyard as comfortable a resting-place
as you can ? That is good, so far as it goes, but that
is not very far. Will that content you ?

Decorate their graves with flowers and evergreens,
and wreaths of pleasant things ? Will that content
you ?

Amuse them with your music, or the singing of your
songs, or the letting off of your oratorical fireworks
among their rotting corpses ? Will that content you ?

Instruct them in doctrines and rescues and salvations
in which they have no share ? Will that content you ?

No ! No ! No ! A thousand times no ! You won't be
content with all that. God has sent you into this dark
valley for nothing less than to raise these doom-struck
creatures from the dead. That is your mission. To
stop short of this will be a disastrous and everlasting
calamity.

What do you say ? It cannot be done ? That is false.
God would never have set you an impossible task. You
cannot do it ? That is false again. For you have
done it before, again and again. There is not an
Officer here who has not called some souls from the
dead. Not one. How many thousands—how many
tens of thousands, in the aggregate, have the Officers
present at this Congress raised from the graves of
iniquity ? Who can tell ?

Go and do it again. Go and look at them. Go and
compassionate them. Go and represent Jesus Christ to
them. Go and prophesy to them. Go and believe for
them. And then shall bone come to bone, and there
shall be a great noise, and a great Army shall stand
up to live, and fight, and die for the living God.

CHAPTER III

THE SPIRIT OF PURITY

SECTION I

*And now we come to the consideration of the message of
the second Spirit.*

Let us recall his words: "O Officers, Officers, the
Great Father has sent me to tell you that if you
would be successful in your campaign against wickedness, selfishness, and fiends, *you must yourselves be
holy*."

*I come now to the task of showing, as far as I am able,
what the plan of life is which God has formed for a
Salvation Army Officer.*

What must an Officer be and do who wants satisfactorily
to fill up the plan God has formed for him? Of
course, there will in some respects be certain striking
differences in that plan. But in the main there will
be remarkable resemblances.

*The first thing that God asks is, that the Officer shall
possess the character He approves.*

You might say the character that He admires. The
very essence of that character is expressed in one
word—*Holiness*.

In the list of qualifications for effective leadership in
this warfare, The Salvation Army has ever placed

Holiness in the first rank. The Army has said, and says to-day, that no other qualities or abilities can take its place. No learning, or knowledge, or talking, or singing, or scheming, or any other gift will make up for the absence of this. You must be good if you are to be a successful Officer in The Salvation Army.

1. Let us suppose that a comrade was to present himself before us this morning, and say, " I am a Salvationist. I want to be an Officer amongst you, and I want to be an Officer after God's own heart; but I am ignorant of the qualifications needed." If I were to ask you what I should say to this brother, I know what your answer would be. You would say, with one voice, " Tell him that, before all else, he must be a holy man."

2. Suppose, further, that I appeared before you myself for the first time at this Congress, and were to say to you : " My comrades, I have come to be your Leader. What is the first, the foundation, quality I require for your leadership? " I know the answer you would give me. You would say, " O General, you must be a holy man."

3. If there were gathered before me, in some mighty building, the choicest spirits now fighting in The Salvation Army the world over—Commissioners and Staff Officers, Field Officers and Local Officers, together with Soldiers of every grade and class; and suppose, further, that standing out before that crowd, I was to propose the question ; " In what position in our qualifications shall I place the blessing of Holiness? " you know what the answer would be.

With a voice that would be heard among the multitudes in Heaven the crowd would answer : " Holiness
must be in the first rank."

4. If this morning I had the privilege of ascending to
   the Celestial City, and asking the assembled angels in
   that mighty temple where, day and night, they worship
   the Great Jehovah : " What position ought Holiness
   to occupy in the qualifications needed by Salvation
   Army Officers in their fight on earth ? " you know that
   angels and archangels, cherubim and seraphim, would
   join with the Seven Spirits that are before the
   Throne with one united shout, loud enough to make
   the ears of Gabriel tingle, and would answer, " *Place
   it first.*"

5. If I could have the still greater privilege of kneeling
   before the intercessory Throne of my dear, my
   precious, my glorified Saviour, and of asking Him
   what position this truth should hold in the hearts and
   efforts of Salvation Army Officers, you know that He
   would answer : " Blessed are the pure in heart."
   Holiness comes first.

6. If, further still, borne on a burning seraph's wings I
   could rise to the Heaven of Heavens, and, like its holy
   inhabitants, be allowed to enter the holy of holies
   where Jehovah especially manifests His glory ; and
   if, prostrate before that Throne, with all reverence
   I should ask the question : " What is the first and
   most important qualification a Salvation Army
   Officer must possess in order to do Your Blessed
   Will ? " you have His answer already. You know
   that He would reply : " *Be ye holy, for I am
   holy.*"

SECTION II

What, then, is that Holiness which constitutes the first qualification of an Officer, and which is asked for by that blessed Spirit of Purity coming from the Throne of God?

In replying to this question I cannot hope to do more than put you in remembrance of what you must already know.

I. *I will, however, to begin with, take the broad ground that Holiness, in the sense in which The Salvation Army uses the word, means entire deliverance from sin.*

I shall explain myself as I go along. But I begin with the assertion that holy souls are saved from sin.

You all know what sin is. And it is important that you should, and that you should be able to define it at a moment's notice to whomsoever may inquire. John says: "All unrighteousness is sin." That is, everything that a man sees to be actually wrong, that to him is sin.

(a) Whether the wrong be an outward act, or an inward thought, or a secret purpose does not affect its character. If the act, or thought, or purpose is wrong to that particular soul it is sin.

(b) Whether the wrong be done in public and blazoned abroad before the world as such, or whether it be committed in darkness and secrecy, where no human eye can follow it, matters not; it is sin.

To be holy, I say, is to be delivered from the commission of sin. Is not that blessed?

II. *To be holy is to be delivered from the penalty of sin.*

"The wages of sin is death." Holy men are fully and freely forgiven. One of the evidences of the possession of Holiness is the full assurance of that deliverance. Salvation from doubt as to this. Is not that blessed?

III. *Holiness includes deliverance from the guilt of sin.*

Sin has a retributive power. At the moment of commission it implants a sting in the conscience, which, in the impenitent man, lights a flame, which, without the application of the Precious Blood, is never extinguished. In Holiness the sting is extracted, and the fire is quenched. Is not that blessed?

IV. *Holiness supposes deliverance from the defilement of sin.*

Sin pollutes the imagination, defiles the memory, and is a filth-creating leaven, which, unless purged away, ultimately corrupts and rots the whole being.

In Holiness all the filth is cleansed away. The soul is washed in the Blood of the Lamb. This is the reason for so much being said in the Bible, and in the experience of entirely sanctified people, about purity of heart. Is not that blessed?

V. *Holiness means complete deliverance from the bondage of sin.*

Every time a sin is committed, the inclination to do the same again is encouraged, and those habits which belong to the evil nature are strengthened until they assume the mastery of the soul, and the soul comes more and more under the tyranny of evil.

In conversion the chains that bind men to sin are broken, but the tendency to evil still lingers behind. In Holiness the bondage is not only entirely destroyed, and the soul completely delivered from these evil tendencies, but is free to do the will of God, so far as it is known, as really as it is done in Heaven. Is not that blessed?

VI. *Holiness supposes the deliverance of the soul from the rule and reign of selfishness.*

The essence of sin is selfishness; that is, the unreasoning, improper love of self.

The essence of Holiness is benevolence. Holy souls are mastered by love, filled with love. Is not that blessed?

Section III

It will be seen, then, that the Officer who enjoys this experience of Holiness will have received power from God to live a life consciously separated from sin.

A man cannot be living in a God-pleasing state if he is knowingly living in sin, or consenting to it, which amounts to the same thing. Let us look a little more closely at this.

I. *Holiness will mean a present separation from all that is openly or secretly untrue.*

Anyone pretending to be doing the will of God, while acting untruthfully or deceitfully in his dealings with those around him, is not only guilty of falsehood, but of hypocrisy.

To be holy is to be sincere.

II. *Holiness means separation from all open and secret dishonesty.*

This applies to everything like defrauding another of that which is his just and lawful due.

III. *Holiness also means separation from all that is unjust.*

Doing unto others as you would that they should do to you, may be truly described as one of the lovely flowers and fruits of purity.

IV. *Holiness means salvation from all neglect of duty to God and man.*

All pretensions to Holiness are vain while the soul is living in the conscious neglect of duty.

1. A holy Officer will do his duty to his Maker. He will love God with all his heart—such a heart as he has, big or little. He will love and worship Him, and strive to please Him in all that he does.

2. A holy Officer will love his neighbour as himself. The law of love will govern his dealings with his family, comrades, neighbours—body and soul.

SECTION IV

That is a beautiful experience which I am describing, is it not, my comrades? And you cannot be surprised that the Spirit of Purity should bring you the message that it is God's plan of life for you.

Upon it let me make a few further remarks.

I. *Holiness is a distinct definite state; a man can be in it or out of it.*

II. *Holiness is enjoyed partially or entirely by all converted people.*

    It can be enjoyed partially. No one would say that every converted man was a holy man, and no one would say that every man who was not perfectly holy was not converted. But I should say, and so would you, that every truly converted man is the master of sin, although he may not be entirely delivered from it.

III. *Then, again, Holiness is a continued growth in sincere souls.*

    With faith, watchfulness, prayer, and obedience, the power of sin diminishes as the days pass along, and the strength of Holiness increases.

IV. *The line which separates a state of entire from a state of partial Holiness may be approached very gradually, but there is a moment when it is crossed.*

    The approach of death is often all but imperceptible, but there is a moment when the last breath is drawn. Just so there is a moment when the body of sin is destroyed, however gradual the process may have been by which that state has been reached. There is a moment when the soul becomes entirely holy— entirely God's.

V. *By perseverance in the sanctified life spiritual manhood is reached, and the soul is perfected in love; that is maturity.*

SECTION V

Let me illustrate the doctrine of Holiness, in its varied aspects, by comparing its attainment to the ascent of a lofty mountain.

Come with me. Yonder is the sacred mount, towering far above the clouds and fogs of sin and selfishness. Around its base, stretching into the distance, as far as eye can reach, lies a flat, dismal, swampy country. The district is thickly populated by a people who, while professing the enjoyment of religion, are swallowed up in unreality about everything that appertains to salvation. They talk, and sing, and pray, and write, and read about it, but they are all more or less in doubt whether they have any individual part or lot in the matter. Sometimes they think they have a hope of Heaven, but more frequently they are afraid that their very hopes are a delusion.

The land is haunted by troubling spirits continually coming and going, that point to past misdoings and coming penalties. Such venomous creatures as hatreds, revenges, lusts, and other evil passions are rife in every direction; while the demons of doubt and despair seem to come and go of their own free will, leading men and women on the one hand to indifference, worldliness, and infidelity, and on the other to darkness and despair. This wild dismal territory we will style "The Land of Uncertainty."

In the centre of this unlovable and undesirable country the mountain of which I want to speak lifts its lofty

head. Call it "Mount Pisgah" or "Mount Beulah,"
or, if you will, call it, "Mount Purity"—I like that term
the best. But whatever you name it, there it is,
rising up above the clouds and fogs of sin, and
selfishness, and doubt, and fear, and condemnation
that ever overhang the swampy land of Uncertainty,
of which I have given you a glimpse.

Look at it. There are some monster mountains in the
natural world, but they are mere molehills alongside
this giant height. Look at it again. Is it not an
entrancing sight? Its lofty brow, crowned with a
halo of glorious light, reaches far upwards towards
the gates of endless day, those living on its summit
having glorious glimpses of the towers and palaces
of the Celestial City. The atmosphere is eminently
promotive of vigorous health and lively spirits. But
its chief claim is the purity of heart, the constant
faith, the loving nature, and the consecrated self-
sacrificing devotion of those who are privileged to
dwell there. It must be a charming place. The
multitudes whose feet have ever been permitted to
tread its blessed heights think so.

But while gazing on the entrancing sight, the question
spontaneously arises: "How can I get there?"
There is evidently no mountain railway nor elevator
on which, while reclining on pillows of ease, and
serenaded by music and song, you can be rapidly
and smoothly lifted up to the blessed summit. Those
who reach that heavenly height must climb what
the Bible calls the "Highway of Holiness." And
they will usually find it a rugged, difficult journey,
often having to fight every inch of the way. But,
once on the celestial summit, the travellers will feel

amply repaid for every atom of trouble and toil
involved in the ascent.

The road to this glorious height passes through
various plateaux or stages which run all round the
sides of the mountain, each different from the other,
and each higher than the one that preceded it.
Travellers to the summit have to pass through each
of these stages. Let me enumerate some of the
chief among them.

I. *To begin with, there is the awakening stage, where the
climbers obtain their first fair view of this holy hill.*

It is here that the desire to make the ascent first
breaks out. This longing is often awakened by
reading various guide-books or holiness advertise-
ments, such as *The War Cry*, or "Perfect Love,"
which set forth the blessedness experienced by those
who make the heavenly ascent. Sometimes the
desire to ascend the holy hill is awakened by the
pure light which every now and then shines from
the summit direct into the travellers' hearts. Or, it
may be their souls are set on fire with a holy
longing to be emptied of sin and filled with love
by the burning testimonies of some of the people who
live up there, but who come down into the valley
every now and then to persuade their comrades to
make the ascent. Anyway, it almost always happens
when those who read these guide-books and listen
to these testimonies begin to search their Bibles and
cry to God for guidance, that a spirit of hunger and
thirst sets in which gives them no rest until they
themselves resolve to take the journey up the side
of this wonderful mountain.

II. *A little higher up, and you reach the starting stage.*

Here those who fully resolve upon seeking holiness of heart first enter their names in the " Travellers' Book." On this plateau I observe that there is a great deal of prayer. You can hear the earnest petitions going up to Heaven, whichever way you turn. And, much prayer as there is, you can hear much singing also. One of the favourite songs commences :—

> " O glorious hope of perfect love !
> It lifts me up to things above,
>   It bears on eagles' wings ;
> It gives my ravished soul a taste,
> And makes me for some moments feast
>   With Jesus' priests and kings."

There is another favourite song which begins :—

> " O joyful sound of Gospel grace !
>   Christ shall in me appear ;
> I, even I, shall see His face,
>   I shall be holy here."

III. *But, still ascending, we come to the wrestling stage.*

Here the travellers are met by numerous enemies, who are in dead opposition to their ever reaching the summit.

I observe that the enemies attack those travellers with doubts as to the possibility of ever reaching the mountain's top, and with scores of questions about apparently conflicting passages of Scripture, and contradictory experiences of Christian people; and, alas ! with only too frequent success, for the whole plateau seems to be strewn with the records of broken resolutions relating to the renouncements of evil habits, tempting companions, and deluding indulgences.

And I observe that lying about are many unfulfilled con-
secrations relating to friends, and money, and children,
and time, and other things; in fact, this stage seems to
be a strange mixture of faith and unbelief; so much
so, that it is difficult to believe that we are on the slopes
of Mount Purity at all.

Here you will find posted on the sides of the rocks in all
directions placards bearing the words : " The things I
would do those I do not, and the things I would not do
those I do, and there is no spiritual health in me."
And up and down you will also see notice-boards
warning would-be travellers not to climb any higher for
fear they should fall again.

But, thank God, while many chicken-hearted souls lie
down in despair on this plateau, or retrace their steps
to the dreary regions below, others declare that there
is no necessity for failure.   These push forward in the
upward ascent, singing as they go :—

> " Though earth and hell the word gainsay,
>   The word of God can never fail ;
>   The Lamb shall take my sins away,
>   'Tis certain, though impossible ;
>   The thing impossible shall be,
>   All things are possible to me."

IV. *So, persevering with our journey, higher up, very much
higher up, we come to the sin-mastering stage.*

This is a glorious plateau.   All who enter it do so by the
narrow passage of repentance towards God, and faith in
our Lord Jesus Christ; receiving in their souls, as
they pass the threshold, the delightful assurance ot
full and free forgiveness through the Blood of the Lamb.

Here men and women walk with heads erect in holy
confidence, and hearts glad with living faith, and

mouths full of joyous song, and eyes steadily fixed on the holy light that streams from the summit of the mount above them. That holy beacon guide is ever calling on them to continue their journey, and ever directing them on the way.

Those who have reached this stage have already made great and encouraging progress; for God has made them conquerors over their inward foes. The rule and reign of pride and malice, envy and lust, covetousness and sensuality, and every other evil thing have come to an end.

They triumph on that account, but the conflict is not yet ended. Sometimes the battling is very severe; but with patient, plodding faith they persevere in the ascent, singing as they go :—

> " Faith, mighty faith, the promise sees,
> And looks to that alone;
> Laughs at impossibilities,
> And cries, ' It shall be done ! ' "

V. *And now, close at hand, is the stage of deliverance, where the triumph is begun.*

And now, ten thousand Hallelujahs, let it be known to all the world around, that once on this plateau the separation from sin is entire ; the heart is fully cleansed from evil; the promise is proved to be true, " They that hunger and thirst after righteousness are filled."

At a great Christian Conference the other day an eminent divine said that The Salvation Army believed in a " perfect sinner," but that he believed in a " perfect Saviour." This, I contend, was a separation of what God has joined together, and which never ought to be put asunder. For, glory be to the Father, glory

be to the Son, and glory be to the Holy Ghost,
The Salvation Army believes, with its Lord, that a
perfect Saviour can make a poor sinner into a perfect
saint.   That is, He can enable him to fulfil His own
command, in which He says : " Be ye therefore perfect,
even as your Father which is in Heaven is perfect."
(*Matthew* v. 48.)

VI. *But there is one plateau higher still which, like a*
tableland, covers the entire summit of the mountain,
and that is the maturity stage.

Here the graces of the Spirit have been perfected by
experience, and faith, and obedience, and the soul does
the will of God as it is done in Heaven, united in the
eternal companionship of that lovely being—*the Spirit*
of Purity.

What do you say to my holy mountain, my comrades ?

Are you living up there ?   Have you climbed as near to
Heaven as that represents ?   If not, I want to make a
declaration which you have often heard before, but
which it will do you no harm to hear again ; namely,
that it is the will of God that you should not only
reach the very summit, but that you should abide there.

SECTION VI

Do you ask why God wills that you should reach and
abide on this holy mountain ?

I. *I reply it is the will of God that you and I, and every*
other Officer in this blessed Army, should be holy for His
own satisfaction.

God finds pleasure in holy men and holy women.   We
know what it is to find pleasure in kindred companions.

It is to like to be near them. To want to live with them, or have them to live with us. It is to be willing to travel any distance, or put ourselves to any inconvenience to reach them. According to the Bible, that is just how God feels towards His faithful people. He finds satisfaction in their doings, and praying, and worship, and song. But when there is unfaithfulness or sin of any kind this pleasure is sadly marred, if not altogether destroyed. In such cases the pleasure is turned to pain, the satisfaction to loathing, and the love to hatred.

Hear what He says of Israel: "In all their affliction He was afflicted, and the angel of His presence saved them; in His love and in His pity He bare them, and carried them all the days of old." If for no other reason than the pleasure it will give to God, don't you think every Officer should, with all his might, seek for Holiness of heart and life?

II. *Another reason why God wants you to live on that blessed mountain is the interest He feels in your welfare.*

He loves you. He has told you so again and again. He has proved His love by His deeds. Love compels the being entertaining the affection to seek the good of its object. He knows that sin is the enemy of your peace, and must mean misery here and hereafter. For this reason among others, He wants to deliver you from it.

You will remember that by the lips of Peter God told the Jews that He had raised up His Son Jesus, and sent Him to bless them by turning every one of them away from his iniquities. That applies to you, my comrades. You have heard it before; I tell it you again. Holiness is the royal road to peace, contentment, and joy for you. The love God bears you, therefore, makes Him ceaselessly long after your Holiness of heart and life. Will you not let Him have His way? Will you not do His will?

III. *God wants every Officer to be holy, in order that through him He may be able to pour His Holy Spirit upon the people to whom that Officer ministers.*

1. The men and women around you are in the dark. Oh, how ignorant they are of God and everlasting things! They cannot see the vile nature of the evil, and the foul character of the fiends that tempt and rule them. They do not see the black ruin that lies before them. So on they go, the blind leading the blind, till over the precipice they fall together. God wants their eyes to be opened. The Spirit can do the work, and through you He wants to pour the light.

2. The men and women around you are weak. They cannot stand up against their own perverted appetites, the charms of the world, or the devices of the devil. God wants to pour the Spirit of Power upon this help-less crowd. But He wants holy people through whom He can convey that strength. He works His miracles by clean people. That is His rule.

There is nothing in the work of the early Apostles more wonderful than the miraculous manner in which they went about breathing the Spirit of Life and Light and Power on the people. But they were fully consecrated, Blood-and-Fire men and women.

What do you say, my comrades? Will you be holy mediums? Do you not answer, " Thy will be done "?

IV. *God wants you to be holy, in order that you may reveal Him to the world by your example.*

Men do not believe in God—that is, the real God—the God of the Bible ; and they do not believe in Him, because they do not know Him.

He seeks to reveal Himself to men in various ways.

1. He reveals Himself through the marvels of the natural world ; and many say they can see God in the sun, and stars, and seas, and trees.

2. He reveals Himself by speaking to men in their own hearts, and many hear His whisperings there.

3. He reveals Himself in His own Book, and some read and ascertain what is His mind there.

But, alas! the great multitude are like children. They require to see and hear God revealed before their very eyes in visible and practical form before they will believe. And to reach these crowds, God wants men and women to walk about the world so that those around, believers and unbelievers alike, shall see the form and hear the voice of the living God ; people who shall be so like Him in spirit, and life, and character as to make the crowds feel as though the very shadow of God had crossed their path. Will you be a shadow of God ?

V. *God wants you to be holy, in order that you may know what His mind is about the world, and about your work in it.*

1. He entertains certain opinions and feelings with respect to it. He has His own plan for saving it.

2. He wants to reveal to you what those opinions and feelings are, and to do this so far as it will be good

for you and those about you. He wants you to know
how you can best fight devils, convict sinners, save
souls, and bless the world.

3. You can have this wonderful knowledge. Paul had
it. He said "We," that is, I, "have the mind of
Christ." God is no respecter of persons. He is as
willing to reveal His mind to you, so far as you need
it, as He was to reveal it to Paul.

4. But to possess this knowledge you must be holy.
Sin darkens the understanding, and hinders the perception of truth. A grain of sand in the eye will
prevent you seeing the most beautiful landscape in
the universe, or the dearest friends you have. It is
with the heart that men see divine things, and an
atom of sin will darken the brightest vision that can
come before you. With a pure heart you can not only
see God's truth, but God Himself. Oh, God wants to
reveal Himself to you. Will you let Him ? But if
He is to do so, you must have a clean heart.

VI. *It is God's will that you should be holy, because He
wants you to be men and women of courage.*

Courage is the most valuable quality in this War. There
are few gifts of greater importance. Only think what
it has enabled the Prophets, the Apostles, and the
Salvation leaders of modern times to accomplish ! How
it covered Moses, and Joshua, and David, and Daniel,
and Paul, and a crowd of others with glory, and
enabled them to conquer men, and devils, and
difficulties of all kinds. I shall have something more
to say about this before I have done.

Courage and Holiness are linked closely together. You
cannot have one without the other. Sin is the very

essence of weakness. A little selfishness, a little insincerity, a little of anything that is evil means condemnation, and loss of courage, which means cowardice and failure.

1. "The wicked flee when no man pursueth." Double-minded people are uncertain, fickle, unreliable in all their ways.

2. "The righteous are bold as a lion." Remember Shadrach, Meshach, Abednego.

VII. *God wants you to be holy, in order that He may do mighty works through your instrumentality.*

I verily believe that His arm is held back from working wonders through the agency of many Officers, because He sees that such success would be their ruin. The spirit of Nebuchadnezzar is in them. He cannot build Babylon, or London, or New York, or anything else by their instrumentality, because He sees it would create the spirit of vainglory and boasting, or of ambition ; make them dissatisfied with their position ; or otherwise curse them and those about them. Look at Saul. What a lesson his history has in it for us all. "When thou wast little in thine own sight wast thou not made the head of the Tribes of Israel ? and the Lord anointed thee king over Israel."

SECTION VII

Now, I may be asked whether some Officers do not fail to reach the higher ranges of the experience I have here described, and the reasons for this.

To this question I reply that I am afraid that it is only too true that some Officers are to be found who are

willing to dwell in the land of uncertainty and feeble-
ness. They are the slaves of habits they condemn in
others. Their example is marred, their powers are
weakened for their work, and, instead of going onward
and upward to the victory they believe so gloriously
possible, they are a disappointment to themselves, to
God, and to their leaders.

If I am asked to name the reasons for their neglect of
this glorious privilege, I would say :—

I. *They have doubts about the possibility of living this
life of Holiness.*

They think there is some fatal necessity laid upon them
to sin—at least a little, or just now and then. They
think that God cannot, or that He will not, or that He
has not arranged to save them altogether from their
inward evils. They know that the Bible says, over and
over again, in a thousand different ways, that the Blood
of Jesus Christ cleanses from all sin ; and they read
God's promise again and again, that He will pour out
His Spirit upon them, to save them from all their idols
and filthiness ; but they doubt whether it is strictly
true, or anyway, whether it applies to them.

And so, tossed to and fro by doubts about this holy
experience, no wonder that they do not seek to realise
it in their own hearts.

II. *Other Officers are kept back from climbing this mountain
by the idea that the experience is not possible to them.*

They say, "Oh, yes, it is good, it is beautiful, I wish I
lived up there. How delightful it must be to have your
peace flow like a river, and your righteousness abound
as the waves of the sea, and to be filled with the Spirit!

But such a life is not for me." They admit the possibility of Holiness in those about them, and occasionally they push it on their acceptance, but they fancy that there is something about their own case that makes it impossible, or, at least, overwhelmingly difficult, for them to attain it.

1. They imagine that there is something in their nature that makes it peculiarly difficult for them to be holy.

    (a) Some peculiar twist in their minds. Some disagreeable disposition.

    (b) Some bad, awkward temper.

    (c) Some unbelieving tendency.

2. Or, they are hindered by something that they suppose to be specially unfavourable in their circumstances— their family.

3. Or, there is something in their history that they think is opposed to their living pure lives—they have failed in their past efforts, etc.

Anyway, there is, they imagine, some insurmountable obstacle to their walking with Christ in white, and, instead of striking out for the summit of the Holy Mountain in desperate and determined search, relying on God's word that all things are possible to him that believeth, they give up, and settle down to the notion that Holiness of heart and life is not for them.

III. *Then, other Officers do not reach this experience because they do not seek it; that is, they do not seek it with all their hearts.*

1. *They do not climb.*

They know that their Bible most emphatically asserts that those who seek heavenly blessings shall find them. No passage is more familiar to their minds or much more frequently on their lips, than the one spoken by Jesus Christ: " Seek, and ye shall find." And they condemn the poor sinner who lies rotting in the sins which will carry him to Hell, because he won't put forth a little effort to find deliverance. And yet, do not some Officers act very much after the same fashion with respect to this blessing ?

In their efforts they are truly sincere, but they are not much more forward for them. They say " It is not for me," and settle down as they were.

The reason for this is not that the promise is not to them. But it is—

(a) Because they have not been thorough in their surrender; or,

(b) Because they have been wanting in their belief; or,

(c) Because they do not persevere ; or

(d) Because they have been mistaken in some past experiences.

2. *Another reason why Officers do not find the blessing is the simple fact that they will not pay the price.*

There is something they will not do ; or there is something they will do; or there is something they will not part with; there is some doubtful thing that they will not give up. The sacrifice is too great. They think they would not be happy, or someone else would not be happy, or something would not be satisfactory; and so they look and look at the Mountain, and long and long, but that is all. They would like to be there, but the price is too great.

3. *Another reason why Officers fail is neither more nor less than their want of faith.*

This, with sincere souls, is by far the most common hindrance. I have something to say about faith further on.

IV. *And, doubtless, the reason that some Officers fail to reach the upper levels of Mount Purity arises out of their mistaken views as to the nature of this experience.*

You have so often heard me dwell on this view of the subject that I despair of saying anything fresh that will help you. But, knowing that I am on ground where truly sincere souls are often hindered, I will make one or two remarks :—

1. *I have no doubt that many fail here by confounding temptation with sin.*

They pray—they consecrate—they believe that they receive, and they rejoice. But by-and-by, when bad thoughts are suggested to their minds, they say to themselves, " Oh, I can't be saved from sin, or I would not have all those wicked thoughts and suggestions streaming through my soul." They confound temptation with sin. Whatever they may say about it, they do not see the difference existing between temptation and sin.

2. *Some Officers are hindered in the fight for Holiness by supposing that purity will deliver them from serious depression, low spirits, and the like.*

With many sincere souls I have no doubt that one of the most serious hindrances in this strife is the confounding of Holiness with happiness, and thinking that if they are holy they will be happy all the time; whereas the Master Himself was a Man of Sorrows, and lived, more or less, a life of grief.

V. *Then there comes the last reason I shall notice, and that is the want of perseverance.*

There are some Officers who *have* been up the Mountain—part of the way, at any rate, if not to the top. But through disobedience, or want of faith, they have no longer the experience they once enjoyed.

VI. *The condition.*

You say to sinners that they are never to give up. I do, at least. So with those who are seeking Holiness. They must persevere or they will never find it.

CHAPTER IV

THE SPIRIT OF DEVOTION

We now come to the message of the third Spirit.

What was his message? What did he say? Listen:
" O Officers, Officers, you must be supremely given up
to the saving of men."

That is the great end for which The Salvation Army
exists.

On this message I remark :—

I. *That every man has some ruling, controlling object in life.*

That is, there is something which forms the chief
attraction of his existence, and influences him most
in all he feels, and says, and does in his everyday
life. Perhaps he does not realise the presence or
power of this force, or the influence it exerts over
him, but it is there all the same.

II. *That object constitutes his ideal.*

All the great things done by men are, in the first
instance, simply ideals; that is, pictures in the mind,
of what they would like to accomplish. And the
realisation of these things by them usually comes
about in something like the following fashion :—

1. They see the thing in imagination.
2. They see that it ought to be done.
3. They see how it might be done.
4. They yearn after its being done.

5. They give themselves up to the doing of it. They say, " It shall be done, and I will do it, if it be possible."

To illustrate what I mean take one or two of the achievements of human genius : the Suez Canal, the Alpine Tunnels.

(a) In the first place, the idea was conceived.

(b) The ways in which the idea might be accomplished were formulated.

(c) The undertaking was resolved upon.

(d) The work was embarked upon.

(e) The task had to be persevered in.

(f) Finally—but not until each of the other stages had been reached—the thing was triumphantly completed.

III. *Now the real object for which The Salvation Army exists is known to us all.*

It is to save men.

Not merely to civilise them. That will follow. Salvation is the shortest and surest cut to civilisation.

Not to educate them. That will follow also; and if it does not, men and women had better live good lives, and get into Heaven at last, than, with heads full of learning, whether secular or religious, finish up in Hell.

Not merely to feed them; that is good, very good, so far as it goes. It is true that in our Social work we feed the starving and house the homeless, but it is only a step towards the purpose we wish to accomplish.

The object is to save men from sin and Hell.

To bring them to God. To bring God to them. To build up the Kingdom of Heaven upon the earth. The end of The Salvation Army Officer is to convert men, to change their hearts and lives, and make them good Saints and Soldiers of Jesus Christ.

IV. *And the Spirit of Devotion, with the crimson Cross inscribed upon his shoulders, who comes to us from the Throne of God, asks for our full consecration to the attainment of this object.*

Not merely that we should admire it, but really and truly choose it as the great end of our lives, and choose it afresh to-day.

For this consecration certain things are necessary :—

1. *The knowledge of its nature.*

Many of you, I have no doubt, offered yourselves for a soul-saving life years ago. You knelt down, as I did, on the day you were converted—perhaps in the very act of being converted, and said, " Lord, help me to live for the salvation of those around me." But you have had much experience since then. You see what it means in the way of tears, of toils, of disappointments, of conflicts, to really follow the Lamb that was slain. What is asked from you by the Spirit from the Throne, is that with this increased knowledge and actual experience you should give yourself up to it again.

2. *This consecration also implies a definite, intelligent offer of yourself to this object without reservation.*

This must be done in the face of all the possibilities before you, with all you really have and are, for better or for worse, and that for all your days.

This consecration involves—

(*a*) The giving up of the pleasures and satisfactions that come from the world around you. For instance :—

(i.) The love of money.

(ii.) The love of pleasure.

(iii.) The love of admiration.

The spirit, rather than the possession, of these things is the snare of the Officer.

(b) This consecration involves also a life of self-denial and toil. There is no other way. I say so.

3. *Now, for the offering of ourselves to live and suffer for the salvation of the world after this fashion, we have the consecration of Jesus Christ as an example.*

Look for a moment at what was involved in the offering He made for us. He foresaw all the humiliation, sorrow, suffering and mockeries that would have to be undergone, and the cruel death that crowned it all. And yet He voluntarily, and deliberately, and gladly gave Himself to the task.

(a) It was voluntary.

(b) It was made without regard to success or failure.

(c) It was actuated by a motive which made it acceptable to God.

4. *I doubt not that many Officers here have followed in His footsteps.*

5. *I hope it has been so with myself.*

I can remember making the offering for the first time sixty years ago. And I have told you before, how that, with the increased knowledge that came with years of suffering and toil, I made the offering in a fuller and more direct manner than at the onset.

6. *Shall we go down before God, and ask ourselves whether after this fashion we are on the Altar this morning ?*

And, if we are not, let us gladly place ourselves there.

CHAPTER V

THE SPIRIT OF HOLY WARFARE

Section I

The fourth Spirit who passed before us, is distinguished from the rest as the Fighting Spirit—the Spirit of Holy War.

In his hand is a flaming sword, and the burden of his message, you will remember, was: "O Officers, Officers, you must fight devils, lies, fleshly indulgences, hardships, disappointments, and everything that sets itself up against God, or that is opposed to the living of a holy life, or which threatens the damnation of man. O Officers, at all risks and consequences, you must fight for God and the salvation of souls."

Let us look at this stirring and deeply interesting message.

I. *And, first of all, what are we to understand by an Officer fighting? What does it mean?*

It means contending with oppositions—difficulties on every hand—doing, or struggling to do, what is hard to be done. When men get what they want without resistance, or loss, or suffering, they do not consider that to be fighting at all. In such circumstances they say, "There was no fight; it was a 'walk over.'" But when they have to struggle, when they have to meet opposing forces, when the conflict is desperate, and calls up all their powers, then they say it was a glorious victory when they win ; and even when they lose, they reckon the loss is less to be mourned over if there was a real, a brave, a determined fight.

II. *Now fighting is the common experience of men in this life.*

I do not know whether it will be so in the next. The general idea is that we shall have everything our own way there. The stream, they think, will run in harmony with our aims and wishes in the Celestial Land. I don't know whether it will be so. It will suit me if it does.

Anyway, fighting is the order of the day in the present world.

Whichever way you look, you will find that nothing is obtained without strife of one kind or another. The plants have to fight to bring their buds into flowers. The trees have to fight to bring their blossoms into fruit. The animals and birds have to fight, not only to avoid being devoured, but for almost every meal they eat. They would starve if they did not fight.

III. *The whole life of man is little but a conflict.*

1. There is the fight to get into the world.
2. There is the fight to keep living when you are in it.

Look at it ; at least one hundred millions of people have to fight to obtain food barely sufficient to keep body and soul together. Even then there are millions— forty millions in India alone—who are seldom free from the sensation of hunger. What a fight is theirs !

3. Look at the fight of still millions more with the diseases that wait to slay them at every turn. To them—indeed, in one sense, to us all—life is one long struggle with death.

4. Look at the fight men make for money. How they resist the claims of health and home, and fight against their own flesh and blood for gold!

5. Look at the fight men make for fame. See how they will sacrifice time, health, friends, nay, life itself, to get what they call a name. How they will glory in dying, as they term it, in the arms of victory.

6. Look at the fight men make for the governments they prefer.

IV. *When you come to religion you will find this principle of conflict still more manifest.*

Here man will get nothing without a fight.

1. There are any number who will get nothing evil without fighting for it. For instance, a man cannot commit sin, mock God, trample on the Blood, resist the Holy Ghost, put out the eyes of his conscience, and die in despair, without fighting and a good deal of hard fighting too.

2. And if this applies to evil things, how much more to good things? Think of the struggle necessary to the attainment of any true spiritual advantage. For example:—

(*a*) The moment a man starts to save his soul, difficulties of all kinds spring up before him. The past—how it holds on to him! The present—what a tearing away, and humbling, and confessing, he

must go through! The future—how black and
empty it often looks!

(b) He will have to fight to keep himself saved.
Enemies will strive to destroy his new-born hope,
and they will follow him to the very gates of
Heaven to drag him down.

(c) He will have to fight if he is to save anyone else.
Men cannot be turned from Satan to God by gentle
phrases and lavender water.   To save men is a
desperate, agonising, wounding business.

(d) Think of the difficulties that have to be surmounted
before a man can have ground for expecting the
" Well done " at the Judgment Throne, or a
victorious crown in Heaven. "Be thou faithful unto
death!"

Do you ever consider what that faithfulness unto death
meant to those to whom the words were first spoken?
The visions of the torture chamber, the wild beasts
in the arena, the Crucifixion, which it called up in
their minds?

V. *This fighting has always been a necessity when anything
out of the common course in the way of the salvation of
men has been sought after.*

1. *Read history.* It would do some of you much more
good than the halfpenny papers.

Go to the prophets!   What a fight Moses had!—
Jeremiah—Jesus Christ—the Apostles—the Martyrs—
the Reformers.   My heart has ached many a time
beyond description when I have read the biographies
of the beautiful spirits who have wept, and fought,
and laid themselves down to die without seeing the
things accomplished for which they have suffered.

2. *Fighting has ever been my own experience.*

From the beginning I have had to contend with earth or Hell, and sometimes with both, for every success God has been pleased to give me.

3. *Fighting has been your experience.*

The day may come when the Salvation ship will glide along the stream of time, laden with souls bound for the Gloryland, without any pulling of the oars, or firing up of the furnaces, without any anxious look-out for stormy breakers ahead. But that time is not yet. Stop rowing, and you will see. Stop feeding the furnace. Stop fighting. You know what the result will be.

If you are saviours of men you must fight. Make up your minds that it is so, and that nothing on earth or in Heaven, human or divine, can change it. The Devil has got possession of the world ; anyway, of the people that dwell in it, and if you want them for Christ and holiness and Heaven, you will have to take your stand, and hold your post, and close with your enemy, and fight for their rescue ; and you may be sure he won't loosen his grip without inflicting all the damage he can upon you who dare to attack him and his prey.

This law is not of my making. I am not responsible for it. I found it in my Bible when I first started to save myself and those around me, and it has been my experience ever since. It is God's plan, and God's plan for us. Have you accepted it? I have. To do so is to go a long way to being happy in it—nay, to do so is to go a long way to being victorious.

SECTION II

Salvation fighting, like all other warfare, seems capable of division into two parts.

These two parts are so closely allied that it is difficult to treat them separately, and yet I must try to do so.

I. *To begin with, there is the work that is necessary to keep the actual fighting going.*

This is, in reality, as much a part of the warfare as the actual attack on the enemy. Still, it often lacks the dash and change and excitement of the latter, and consists mainly of hard, monotonous out-of-sight toil.

Such labour as this, however, is common to all warfare.

1. Not a hundredth part of the time of the military soldier, whether officer or private, is occupied with the excitement of battle, even in war time. All his other time and energies are taken up with doing uninteresting, monotonous, out-of-sight work.

There is the drill. What an uninteresting set of repetitions that usually is! The guard—the watch, by day and by night. The long, weary marching, or the endless journeys by rail or ship; the carrying to and fro of ammunition; the preparation of the food: rough and ready as it often is, both officer and soldier are frequently glad if they can get any to prepare; the clothes to be kept whole; the cleaning of the weapons; the reporting of every movement of the enemy and of his own force; the doing of all these things must be very uninteresting, but none of them can be dispensed with.

2. *Take commercial warfare*, where you have much the same thing in both principle and practice.

Think of the unceasing night and day work necessary to keep a railway running. Think of the monotonous work necessary to keep the doors of a big bank open, to construct a railway, make a tunnel, or a dock, or to conduct any similar operation. Work, work, work, is the order, the necessity of these and all similar transactions. They cannot be carried on without work.

3. *This has applied to my own warfare.*

It is very easy to make a mistake here. You see me on the platform, you hear me talking to the thousands, etc. You say, "Ah, The General has a rare old time of it. He is sustained by a whirl of holy excitement. Bless him! Let us give him another volley! How different is his lot from mine!" But behind the scenes, out of sight, my body, and heart, and brain have to grind on night and day, and that with as little cessation as is the lot of any Officer in this Hall.

I have not had a furlough for fifteen years. I have just decided to take a month on a motor car, but I am going to hold three meetings a day! But even if you still think my lot is more favourable, Lieutenant, than yours, in this respect, you must wait till you have ground on for fifty or sixty years as I have been enabled to do.

Every man who wants to really lead must be willing to grind. It cannot be done without. It never has been. It never will be.

4. *This rule applies to you, my comrades, if you are to be of any use to the world.*

You cannot be useful and successful without doing this uninteresting, out-of-sight work, and plenty of it.

5. *You cannot have a battle without it.*

Think of the work some battles have involved. The monstrous toil of thousands of men for months, nay, years, in preparing for it. It is said that the Japanese had been preparing for the struggle with Russia for ten years.

Some of you look upon this Congress—the public part of it—as a battle; and so it truly is, but think of the out-of-sight work that has been done to get ready for it; that had to be done if the battle had to be fought. Without the work you could not have had this glorious fight.

II. *The Officer must do this kind of work, in order to prepare his Soldiers to fight.*

That is, he must deal with them as Soldiers. He must train them. One great difference between an Officer and a Soldier is the amount of Training that has been received. Not merely as hearers, supporters, contributors, collectors, admirers, but as Soldiers. How often have I told you this? I will tell you once more.

III. *Every Officer ought to be encouraged by the consideration of the wonderful things that this monotonous kind of work has already accomplished.*

It is true that the public aggressive warfare has been largely instrumental in securing the remarkable success with which we have been favoured, but the steady out-of-sight labour has greatly assisted, not only in making that public fighting effective, but in conserving and consolidating the results.

Take, as a definite illustration of my meaning, the work that has been involved in one branch of Army effort—the creation of our eighteen thousand Bandsmen. An immense amount of toil has been entailed in :

1. Getting them saved.
2. Watching over them.
3. Selecting them.
4. Teaching them.
5. Keeping them faithful.

Then look at the work they have had to do themselves in learning :

1. How to make the sounds.
2. How to read the notes.
3. How to keep the time.
4. The Italian and French words.

I heard of a drummer who used to take the drum to bed with him, and practise in the small hours of the morning.

SECTION III

Now let me take the aggressive side of a Salvation Army Officer's life and warfare; and by that I mean the unflinching and fearless attack upon wrong-doing and wrong-doers.

He must fight evil wherever and whenever he finds it. He must not let it alone. Tempted, though he will be, to say, " Let us have peace in our time, O Lord," he must unsparingly attack it. He must bring to that attack a determined mind, and a bold and loving heart.

There will be two directions in which Officers will generally be required to meet and grapple with evil, and its consequences.

I. *The first of these will be in the hearts and lives of the people entrusted to their care.*

There is a needs be that offences come. Jesus Christ said so. They cannot be prevented. They will be found, more or less, in every Command. Constituted as human nature is, even *saved* human nature, there will always be some trouble or evil to be faced by every real Commanding Officer and lover of souls.

1. *The Officer must help his people in their fight with their own personal trials, temptations, and sins.*

He should make them feel that he is a real stand-by in their difficulties. Many of them are sorely tried.

2. *Look at their depressions!*

How many of them go down into low spirits and despondency, and feel like giving up the struggle as hopeless. The Officer must fight that depression; He must encourage them, show them the bright side of the cloud, have patience with them. The balance of many a battle has been turned by one kind word, and thousands have been strengthened in the conflict with this kind of trial by the feeling that their leaders would cheer them up.

3. *Look at the afflictions of the people!*

How few homes there are without sickness, and how few hearts without sorrow. Disappointment and loss and separation seem to be the common rule of the great mass. Look at the trials of parents in their children, and the trials of children in their parents. Remember the loneliness and separation of some wives and some husbands. And how many of our people all over the world are set alone in families and households far from their own loved ones.

Now an Officer's duty is to help them in these trials. He is to get to know them, and give such advice as is helpful to them; stand firm as a rock by the side of those who are suffering, so that they may lean on him. In short, he must help them to fight their trials.

4. *Look at the temptations of our people !*

Who can tell how many thousands of them have to struggle with the remnants of old habits, and the fiery temptations which come by old companionships, calling them back to evil ?

Look how many there are whose sorest temptations come to them through their families—young people especially, living in families all opposed to goodness. The constant butt of sarcasm and ridicule, and often tried beyond endurance. Consider how many of our Soldiers work amidst conditions which are simply abominable. Surrounded by blasphemy and filthy talk, or by the steady repulsive indifference of pride and hate. It is the Officer's business to help them to fight these evils.

5. *Look at the spiritual foes of our people.*

(*a*) Their weak natures. Do they not require help ? It is no use blaming them. There they are, poor, wobbling, feeble creatures, many of them so by birth.

(*b*) Look at their wicked natures. It is no use disguising the fact. Many hearts seem unfavourable to the work of God's grace—stony, selfish natures. Twisted, awkward creatures, who go all through life taking everything and everybody awry. What a foe to a man's soul such a nature must be !

(c) Devils.

Do we sufficiently realise that the devils are told off to destroy, and trip up, and overthrow ? Every Officer here has some people under his care who are, this very day, being dogged, and pestered, and watched, and followed, with sleuth-like tenacity, by the fiends of Hell who are seeking to get hold of them.

Now I say you are to fight these difficulties. You have not been saved and washed, and sanctified and called, and set apart and promoted, merely to record them, or to moan over them.

All this has been done for you, that you may fight them with your own hands, and with your own hearts, and with your own strength of mind and soul. You must grapple with these evils. How can you better do this than you have done it in the past ? That is the question. How can you more really conform to the command of the spirit of war than hitherto ? Well, I can only give you one or two simple counsels, which I have found very useful in my own efforts to help the people around me.

(i) *Make them believe that victory is possible.*

And to do this, the most important of all is, that you should believe it yourself. Never let go your faith in the possibility of God's final triumphing in any soul you have to deal with. Say to yourself in the face of every weakness and disappointment, and say to them : " God *can ;* God *is* able." Keep a smiling face. Many a battle has been won by the confident mien of the general's countenance. Many a poor soul has been plucked from despair and damnation by the smiling face of his Captain in the hour of difficulty.

(ii) *Do not let temporary defeats discourage them, or prevent them trying again.*

Forget the things which are behind. Show them how to do it. Never mind the disappointment you feel yourself. Do not show the white feather.

(iii) *As far as possible deal with individuals.*

Give them personal advice which can only come by individual contact. Give all the instruction you can from your own experience.

Stand up to families and employers who persecute your people. Visit them. Let them see your hearty interest in those for whom you plead. Sometimes you might take a deputation with you. Pray with them.

II. *The second way in which Officers will be required to meet and grapple with evil and its consequences will be in fighting the enemies of God and man who are raging and triumphing outside our camp.*

We all know the difference between the spirit of the Church and the spirit of The Army in this respect.

The Church is ordinarily occupied with herself. As a rule, her clergymen, or pastors, or priests, do not feel any particular responsibility for the welfare of the people outside their own particular circle.

It is true that by Missions—Home and Foreign—there is some attempt to reach the perishing multitudes, but these efforts soon crystallise into little churches themselves, becoming as formal and as separate from the perishing crowds as the mother who gives them birth.

It is also true that, stimulated in a measure by the example of The Salvation Army, there has been, of late years, a great breaking out in Revival Efforts, Social Schemes, Forward Movements, and the like.

But, after all, the Church, as a whole, has little sympathy, and takes only a feeble part in these extraordinary efforts. And, if roused for the moment to consider the awful condition of the majority of mankind, she soon tires of toil and sacrifice on their account, and falls back upon her normal condition, which mainly consists in taking care of herself. She sustains her operations by her own gifts, and keeps up her membership by her own sons and daughters. But for the addition that comes to her from her own children and Sunday Schools, she would dwindle away and die.

This method of sustentation is right, so far as it goes, and The Army will act on the same rule more than ever in the future.

SECTION IV

I. *You see the fiends of Hell, devouring the happiness and lives and souls of the people by thousands.*

I believe many of you do. I would to God you all did!

You can see the Devil going about like a roaring lion. Are you willing to let those fiends feed on the bodies and souls of the people in peace? No! Then you must fight.

II. *Again, you see around you the giant fiends of earth doing the same deadly work.*

Fouler fiends, I was going to say, are these fiends of earth than the fiends of Hell. There is pride; there is malice; there is worldliness in its unnumbered forms; selfishness; covetousness; drunkenness and the drunkard makers; harlotry and the harlot makers; infidelity and the infidel makers; hypocrisy and the hypocrite makers; war and the war makers.

What will you do with them? What is the will of God that you should do with them? What does the message you have received from the Throne of God, this very Congress, say that you should do with them?

You must fight them.

III. *You must fight for the absolute rescue of these poor and deluded victims.*

Helping them is very good in many ways; but I am not quite sure of its advantages, if you leave them, still gripped fast in the clutches of the Devil. Anyway, you must not be content with—

1. Merely ameliorating their temporal miseries, or of delivering them from them.

2. Instructing them.

3. Changing their outward habits.

4. Attaching them to your Corps, or making them helpers in your work.

IV. *You must not stop short of actually rescuing them from their sins, and changing their hearts, and making them into Soldiers of Jesus Christ.*

And how are you to do this?

1. *You must do this by making the people know the truth.*

As regards God. Bring Him home to them. Make them realise that He is, and that His nature is Love, Justice, Purity.

By making them realise the truth as regards sin. I have
said something to you already about the search-light
which He will give you. Now you must turn it on to
people's consciences, and make them feel something
of what He feels about their sinning against Him.

By making them feel the truth as regards Judgment,
Heaven, and Hell. All around you there is growing up
a great peril of unbelief on these questions. You must
fight it. You must make men feel and see that there is
a Heaven, that there is a Hell, and that there will
certainly be a great Judgment Bar, before which they
must stand.

You must make them know the truth as regards the
sacrifice of Jesus Christ and its sufficiency. Publish
abroad the efficacy of the precious Blood, and all the
blessings that flow from salvation.

2. *You must do this by using all the means in your
power to awaken men to their danger.*

Men sleep on the very verge of Hell. You must fight
to awaken them. They walk about in their sleep,
and live as in a dream. Their business, their pleasure,
their sorrows, their miseries, hold them fast in a
slumber nearly as deep as death itself—nay, they are
dead while they live.

You must awaken them, You know how you awaken
people ordinarily who are asleep. You rush in upon
them. You make them feel, hear, see something.
You startle them, you change the current of their
thoughts, you inflict a passing pain, or do something
entirely unexpected. So here with these sleeping
souls. You must do something. You must come in
upon them in their business, and amidst their amusements. You must shake them in their sorrows, and

in their bitter miseries.　Startle them out of the fatal
stupor in which they stand all unheeding on the brink
of a burning Hell.　Fight the sleeping sickness.

3. *You must fight to make men repent.*

Not merely to listen to you and wish they were better,
but to be sorry, angry with themselves, broken-
hearted because they have been so wicked and so
bad as to lift themselves up against God.　He willeth
not the death of a sinner, but that all men should
repent.　Your business is to fight for their repentance.

You must do all this—amongst other means, by your
own talking and appeals.　Especially will this apply
to your meetings.　A satisfactory meeting, in my
opinion, has always meant a real fight—a regular
struggle to get something done at somebody for their
good in time and in eternity.

This applies no matter how large or how small the
meeting may be.　It should imply :

(a) A real effort to get the Devil out of some soul—
young or old, rich or poor; to get God and goodness in; or to make somebody fight for Him who
did not fight before.

(b) This aim distinguishes me.

(c) This aim distinguishes you.

(d) This aim distinguishes The Army from the Churches
around us.　People they say fly from us.　They
won't come again.　They are afraid of the attack.
They don't like the plain dealing about their wrong-
doing—the being brought face to face with their
own conscience.　This is true.　No doubt they do.
They fly from God.　They fly from Jesus Christ.
They quench the Spirit.

What then ? We must fly after them. Anyway, we must go on with the work of rescue. The Dane who said, " My God! I never want to hear the Chief speak again." Shall the Chief hold back the truth, or soften his presentation of it because it cut into this man's guilty conscience. A thousand times, *no !* I say. What do you say ?

Does somebody here to-day ask me, " How shall I get the Spirit which produces this love and life of fighting?" Well, I would say, choose Him. Go down before Him here if you have never done it before and say, "O Blessed Spirit of the living God, Thou enemy of wrong, Thou who art the Eternal and unchanging foe of that great destroyer, Sin; Thou who hast drawn the sword, never to sheathe it again until Thine enemies become Thy footstool; I take my place beside Thee; I choose Thee as the captain of my soul; I give myself up to Thee, to drink in Thy Spirit, to conquer or to die."

CHAPTER VI

THE SPIRIT OF TRUTH

Section I

We now come to the fifth Spirit—the shining Spirit of Truth. What was his message?

Hear him again: "O Officers, Officers, your work is to make men know the unchanging and the unchangeable truth about the love of God, the efficacy of the Blood of the Lamb, the accursedness of evil, the cruelty of the Devil, the terrors of the Great White Throne, the joys of Heaven, and the horrors of the damnation of Hell. To do this you must be filled with the Light yourselves."

I. *You must know the things that are essential to a right and profitable discharge of the duties of your position.*

II. *Men perish in ignorance.*

You are sent to instruct them in the things that belong to their peace.

1. *Men are blind.*

You must make them see. This is your duty.

(*a*) You must make them see the evils of sin.

(*b*) You must make them see the dangers of damnation. They go over the precipice because they don't see it.

(c) They don't see the preciousness of the Divine favour. You must show it to them.

(d) They don't see the beauty of believing. You must prove it to them.

2. *Men are deaf.*

You must make them hear the voice of God calling them to His arms, imploring them to come and help.

3. *Men are insensible to the charms of salvation.*

You must make them feel. This is your business.

III. *To do this effectively you must be true yourselves.*

1. You must yourselves know the meaning, and importance, and reason of the truths you proclaim to others. All the world over the cry is for more secular knowledge. Voices can be heard in all directions crying: " Give us more scientific knowledge, give us more technical knowledge, give us more knowledge about commerce and trade, give us more mechanical knowledge, give us more military knowledge."

The cry is being attended to, and everywhere men and women and children are hard at work with the prevalent answer to it. Men are learning how to construct machinery, explore the mazes of science, make fortunes, etc.

There is no denying the fact that twenty years ago the Russians would have swept the Japanese off both sea and land in a very short time. What has made the difference? *Knowledge.* The Japanese now know as much, man for man, as the Russians, if not more.

All that is necessary to be believed in order to your own salvation and the salvation of those about you with whom you have to deal, is already revealed. You do not require to study in order to discover the foundation principles that have to do with the salvation of the world. They are there, revealed and unalterable, for you to examine, receive, believe, and obey.

(a) For instance, we do not require any new revelation as to the Being of God, His nature and attributes, and the purpose He has in view in His dealings with men. Perhaps Enoch, and Moses, and John knew all that we know, and all that can be known down here.

(b) We do not require any new revelation respecting the person of Jesus Christ, His compassion, His miracles, His sacrifice, His resurrection and ascension, together with the virtue of His precious Blood.

(c) We do not require any new revelation respecting the Holy Ghost. His ability to purify and inspire the soul of man with the fire of burning love for a dying world is manifested.

(d) We do not require any new revelation about salvation itself, or the conditions on which it may be won, in order to share in the enjoyment of all its benefits.

(e) We do not require any new revelation about the consequences of the acceptance or rejection of God's mercy. We may have yet more light spread upon these joys and sorrows, but the great unalterable facts are there to accept or reject.

IV. *But while we do not require any new revelation about Salvation, or its Author or character, there is room, nay, an absolute necessity, for definite improvement in the methods employed for its promulgation.*

The corn and oil carried from one part of the world to another are neither better nor worse than those precious commodities were in the Saviour's days.

But there is a great improvement in the means of transit. I guess it would take Jacob's sons a longer period to traverse those couple of hundred miles between Canaan and the city of the Pharaohs than it now takes to bring corn to England from the western prairies of the United States or the north-western portions of Canada, a distance of five thousand miles or more.

Suppose there had been anything like an equivalent advance in the method of spreading abroad the Bread of Life to that which has been made in the trans-mission of the natural staff of existence, the whole world would have been filled long ago with the song : " Glory to God in the highest."

We must improve.

It is true that great improvement has been made from time to time. For instance :—

1. The Apostles were a great advance on the Prophets in the publication of Divine mercy.

2. The Salvation Army is undoubtedly a great improve-ment on the ordinary Christian organisations, both past and present, in the direction of conveying the saving knowledge of Divine grace to the sons of men. This is proved by her works, and admitted by the most thoughtful and experienced friends of God.

3. I trust that I am an improvement in the same direction upon many teachers and preachers who have preceded me. At least my people think so.

4. You are an improvement in the knowledge that makes men know and obey God, or you would not be here.

5. Greater improvement still must be possible. Surely, surely, we have not reached finality.

SECTION II

Besides this improvement in the united operations of The Army, we want improvement in the individual Officer.

With still further improvement in Officers we shall have improvement in every other direction. O Officers, Officers, you are my great concern. Were I dying before your eyes in this very Hall I should call on you, by all that was sacred on earth and in Heaven, to improve yourself.

With many Officers there is unquestionably great advance. The Commissioners are improved, and so are the Staff generally. They are certainly dressed better, and from appearance I should judge they weigh much heavier.

The Field Officers are improved, they do not appear to weigh any less. But there are other directions in which I think there is room for great improvement.

On this subject there is room for a year's talking. But I will content myself with simply telling you something of what I would do for my own improvement, if I could go back to the days of my youth.

I. *I would take more care of my health.*

Many of you have heard me speak about health, and tried earnestly and successfully to forget, at the earliest opportunity, the common-sense counsels I gave you on those occasions. Others, I have reason to know, profited by them; but alas! they are only the exceptions.

I am able to speak to you experimentally. I have had difficulties on this matter all through my life. But until a serious attack of fever when I was sixteen, I scarcely knew what a day's sickness was. As far as my own feelings went I did not know that I had any digestive organs until then. I went on raging and tearing, outdoors and in, night after night, with long business hours, day after day, and long walks to preaching engagements on a Sunday. Then the breakdown came, and I have suffered in consequence ever since. Nevertheless, I am still in the same work. I am not going to say " Follow my example." I have no revelation, but my experience is an object-lesson which should, I think, be studied.

II. *I would cultivate the habit of observation as a means of obtaining information.*

Not lazily allowing things to pass before my gaze without looking into them and asking myself, " How far can I profit by them ? " But carefully studying men and women and children of all classes and conditions with a view of learning something from their badness and their goodness, their joys and their sorrows.

III. *I would ask questions as I went along when I saw things that I did not understand.*

And not let everything pass as a matter of course unworthy of my thought and understanding.

IV. *I would seek to strengthen my power of thought.*

Thinking is one great want of The Salvation Army at the present day. Officers do not sufficiently say to themselves, " Is there no way of doing this work more effectively ? How can I improve on this plan ? How can I better understand this truth ? "

V. *I would do everything that I reasonably could to improve my memory.*

Consider what some people have done with their memory. For instance, Spurgeon. Memory, like every other faculty, may be cultivated. You may readily, if you will inquire, get suggestions as to the cultivation of memories. But after all there is nothing like practice. One of the common snares is trying to do too much.

I am not going to say that by any process you can improve your faculty to this extent. Still, a great deal can be done if you will make the effort, and you will find that the results will pay you well. Naturally, I don't think I excel with respect to this gift. Yet people often express their surprise at the extent to which I can call up things that I have heard and seen in the past.

VI. *I would cultivate to its very utmost the habit of improving my time.*

One man says, "Time is flying, what can I do?" And there is an end of it, so far as he is concerned. Another lets the moments creep away without noticing any useful employment, without noticing their flight, or without feeling any regrets in consequence. This cultivation implies—

1. Some perception of the value of time.
2. The resolution to make the most of it.
3. What is most important of all, the habit of seizing the stray moments as they pass. This I have endeavoured to do until now. To be unemployed in some useful manner is absolute misery to me. But

if I had my time to go over again I would go further
still in this direction; in fact, I am doing so every
day. I recommend the same to you.

Thomas Cromwell is said to have committed to memory
the New Testament whilst travelling from London to
Rome.

VII. *I would seek that knowledge which before all
others seemed most likely to be useful to me in my
work of saving souls, and building up the Kingdom of
Heaven.*

It cannot, in my opinion, be wise to spend time and
energy in acquiring knowledge which has little or no
bearing on the main object to which your lives have
been specially consecrated, and for want of which souls
are dying.   Especially must this be the case with an
Officer who is palpably ignorant on subjects of vital
importance, intimately associated with successful
labour, or who has capacities, which, if instructed,
might do work of unutterable value.

The wandering mind.   How few exercise control over
their thoughts.   I think I have to some extent been
obedient to this law myself, but I would attend to
it far more thoughtfully if I had my days to go over
again.

VIII. *I would read my Bible with greater regularity,
and more carefully store my mind with its prominent
histories, its most striking facts, and its most important
teachings than I did in the days of my youth.   That is a
wonderful Book.*

The late Marquis of Salisbury, for many years Prime
Minister of this country, writing to a correspondent

who had inquired his views of the New Testament, said:—

"Everyone has their own point of view from which they look at things. To me the central point is the Resurrection of Christ, which I believe; first: because it is testified to by men who had every opportunity of seeing and knowing, and whose veracity was tested by the most tremendous trials, both of energy and endurance, during long lives; secondly, because of the marvellous effect it has had upon the world. To anyone who believes the Resurrection of Christ, the rest presents little difficulty. No one who has that belief will doubt that those who were commissioned by Him to speak—Paul, Peter (Mark), John—carried a Divine message. St. Matthew falls into the same category. St. Luke has the warrant of the generation of Christians who saw and heard the others. That is the barest and roughest form the line which the evidence of the inspiration of the New Testament has always taken in my mind. But intellectual arguments, as you well know, are not to be relied upon in such matters alone."

Another Prime Minister of England, the Right Honourable W. E. Gladstone, wrote a book upon the subject of the Inspiration of the Bible, to which he gave the title of "*The Impregnable Rock of Holy Scripture.*"

IX. *I would seek more industriously, as I had opportunity, to gather up in the storehouse of memory the leading occurrences in the world's history.*

X. *I would read with more care the biographies, and study the writings, of the men and women who have most closely walked with God, lived the holiest lives, been the most famous students of the science of soul-saving, and proved themselves to be the most successful heroes in that all-important warfare.*

Section III

Then I would more carefully cultivate the art, science, gift, or whatever you may call it, of speaking to men on the infinitely important subject of Salvation.

Of the importance of this gift there is no need for me to speak to you. The Officer in The Salvation Army who does not see the grandeur of the opportunity he possesses of speaking to men about God and Eternity, and who does not earnestly desire to qualify himself for the effective discharge of the duty, must be altogether unworthy of his post.

God has given me some ability as a public speaker. I have already referred to the tens of thousands I have been permitted to see kneeling broken-hearted at the mercy-seat. These thousands of souls all impressed, nay, deeply convicted and saved, bear witness to the power I possess as a salvation preacher. The Salvation Army itself is, to some extent, an evidence of my ability to talk to the hearts of men. Am I glorying in myself? God forbid. I say these things for your sake, to justify me in advising you in listening to my counsel.

Now how did I acquire this ability to talk? Beyond question I possess some natural gifts—they came into the world with me. But for the encouragement of every young Officer here to-day, I want to say that the bulk of my little ability as a public speaker has come by the way of industrious, persistent, self-denying cultivation. My soul was drawn out in desire after the power to speak of the things of God to the hearts of men in the earliest hours

of my first love. I yearned after it with an unutterable yearning, and that long before I had any
reason to believe that this gift would ever be mine.
I made up my mind to seek it before I had been
saved twelve months, and at once set myself to
the task.

I have fought hard in this pursuit. Few Officers here
have had more disappointments, and depressions,
and temptations in their talking than I have myself.
But I have persevered, and I am still following
on as earnestly as ever in the pursuit. But I
never expect to reach satisfaction with my attainment
in this respect, and so shall still fight on to gain greater
ability to persuade men to abandon the path of evil and
seek God ; to save souls, and help Jesus Christ to win
the world, till I drop into the grave, and exchange
earth for Heaven.

Does anyone ask me how I have attained what ability as
a talker I do possess? I answer that I am coming to
the opinion that every man must learn for himself how
to talk, if ever he learns at all. However, I will give
you a few hints. And I will do so by describing the
things which, taken together, are likely to make a
successful Salvation Army talker.

I. *He must be actuated by right, God-pleasing motives.*
Almost everything will depend on the character of the
motives which carry him to the people.

  1. *His aim must be above all self-seeking—vain, man-
  pleasing feelings.*
  If he is after the praises of men, or the rewards of this
  world, he cannot expect the Holy Ghost to second
  his efforts.

2. *His motive must be beyond the mere desire to preach the truth or explain the Bible, or remind his hearers of what they already know.*

In these things there is no practical application of truth to the present need of those before him.

3. *His aim must be to bless them by saving them in some form or other from sin, and leading them on to a more earnest, self-denying life for God and the salvation of others.*

II. *Having this aim, much will depend on preparation for the right discharge of the duty.*

There are different views on the subject of preparation for the platform. I will tell you mine. Some think that no preparation is needed ; that it is wrong to pray and study as to the message you are to deliver. "Open your mouth wide," they say, "and God will fill it." That is not my view, and it has never been my practice. To those who entertain these notions I would say :—

If you are on such good terms with the Blessed Spirit that He will fill your pitcher with the living water without any trouble to yourself, very good. I have always had to draw mine out of the well, and very deep I have often found that well to be; and very hard pumping it has usually been to get out what I have wanted. It is true that many of my most impressive, most convincing, and most effective thoughts, illustrations, and appeals have come to me on the platform at the moment they were needed. But, as a rule, I have had to work my brain, search my Bible, look over my experience, call up to memory the incidents of the past, and then, with infinite pains, cast these thoughts, etc., into shape, and fix them into such order as has seemed most likely to produce the effect I have desired on the hearts of my hearers.

It is true that in nature every now and then you will have a good crop in your garden for which little or no preparation has been made; but is that any rule why you should give up cultivating altogether? Just so with talking.

Do you ask me how I would advise an Officer to go about preparing an address?

As I have said, I have tried before, and with little success, and now I have little time. Here, however, is an outline:—

1. *Choose your subject.*

Your subject should in some way be—

(*a*) Applicable to the present need of the people who who will hear you. Very much alike.

(*b*) Practical—something that can be turned to present account.

(*c*) Interesting, if possible. Something that will catch the ear, and move the curiosity at once.

(*d*) Within your ability to handle.

(*e*) One on which you can ask God's endorsement and blessing.

2. *Having chosen your subject, consider the form in which you can best present it.*

3. *Explain the truth you present in the simplest language you can find.*

The common error of talking over people's heads. Use your own language, such words, that is, as you are accustomed to employ when expressing yourself in the affairs of your everyday life.

4. *Make certain that you are understood by the most ignorant of your hearers ; illustrate freely.*

The simpler your illustrations are the better. Illustrations that need explanation are next door to useless.

5. *Support what you have to say, so far as you can, by facts.*

Nevertheless, don't drag yourself in more than advisable.

6. *Apply the truth preached as you go along.*

7. *Appeal for action corresponding to what you have been urging on your hearers there and then.*

"Now is the accepted time."

Section IV

And now that you have got your topic, and prepared yourself for it, what about the manner of its delivery?

Well, I have been describing it as I have gone along. Another word may be useful.

I will tell you what I think you should aim at:—

1. *Aim at naturalness. Be yourself.*

Don't mimic anyone else. If you are yourself you will be sure to be interesting. This is difficult, strange to say, but you must struggle after it.

2. *Aim at distinctness.*

As a rule, your hearers will not be at much trouble to listen to you, and therefore must know what you are saying, that is, what you mean, without having to attend very closely. That is, if they are to be any forwarder for your talk.

3. *Aim at directness. Talk to the people.*

Beauty is said to be the eye of the beholder. I get my inspiration out of the eyes of those who listen to me.

4. *Be in dead earnest.*

This is the crowning quality of all Salvation talking. You have all heard of the orator, who, when asked what were the chief properties needed for effective public speaking, replied: "Action, action, action." I can hardly believe it, but if anyone proposed the question to me in its reference to a Salvation Army speaker, I should say: that, given something to say, the all-important thing needed is—earnestness, earnestness, earnestness.

Now that is my counsel with respect to your improvement. Standing here, as I do, with nearly sixty years of experience and observation behind me; with my mind open before Heaven to receive further light direct from Him or through any medium ; and desiring, with an unutterable desire, to rightly interpret the mind of God as it may affect the important questions we have been considering, I do not think that any more useful or practicable advice could very well be given you. May God help you to act upon it.

5. *Spread the light.*

You have it. What is the use of a sun that does not shine?

CHAPTER VII

THE SPIRIT OF FAITH

SECTION I

*And now we come to the sixth of these wonderful Spirits—
the Spirit of Faith.*

*Each Spirit that has passed before us from the Throne of
God, in this Congress, has brought us a message of
unutterable importance, but none has a closer bearing
upon our holiness, usefulness, and joy than the one whose
message we now come to consider, viz., the Spirit of Faith.*

It is important to us personally; to God's Kingdom;
to the whole world; and to our work in the world.

Let us hear that message again: " O Officers, Officers,
you cannot do without me. Listen to my words. If you
treasure them in your hearts, and carry them out in your
lives, you shall be conquerors. If you neglect them,
you will be defeated, no matter how brave you are in
other things. You must take the inscription on my
banner as your life-long motto—*You must believe.*
You must do it night and day, in sorrow and in joy,
in defeat and in victory, living and dying. *You must
be men and women of faith.*"

*Let us proceed to consider this counsel. And, first, I
remark:—*

I. *How desolate we should all be without faith, no matter
what else we possessed, either of this world or any other.*

1. It is only by means of faith that we can obtain any satisfactory assurance of the existence of God. To be without faith, then, is to be without God. That is, "without hope, and without God in the world." It is true that there are voices in nature and voices in Providence, and voices within us, and voices that come from the good and true around us that are ever saying, "There is a God;" but unless we believed their testimony all would be in vain. Anyway, they would do little more than land us in the desolate swamps of uncertainty on this all-important question.

2. But, while accepting the fact of the Being of God, it is only by faith that we know that He has spoken to man. Therefore, to be without faith would be equivalent to being without a Bible. What that loss would be it is difficult to conceive. Suppose we woke up to-morrow morning, and found that every Bible at present in existence had been taken out of the world? Or suppose—which would amount to the same thing—that, all at once, we discovered that every page in our Bibles had become blank paper? What a mourning and lamentation there would be, and justly so. People who had never thought it worth the trouble to read their Bibles would wail. People who had read, and disbelieved would mourn. Even people who had read and disobeyed would feel they had lost what could never be replaced.

And yet, to have the Bible without a living faith in its revelations, and a positive obedience to its precepts, is really worse than having none at all. For he that reads his Maker's will, and believes it not, is not likely to obey; and to know and not do is to be visited with the greater condemnation.

3. It is only by faith that we can obtain any assurance of an existence beyond the grave.

To be without faith is, therefore, equal to being without immortality. Men may make guesses, and indulge in aspirations in favour of a future life, but without faith there is no assurance on the subject. They are left to imagination. It is only by faith that we know that we are of any greater value than the beasts of the field—anyway, so far as existence after death is concerned.

4. It is only by means of faith that we can obtain any satisfying assurance of the favour of God.

5. Without faith there can be no real peace amidst the trials, conflicts, and agonies of life. All the attempts of philosophy to manufacture consolation in such circumstances have proved a dead failure. They have been tried. They are a mockery, a delusion, and a snare.

6. To be without faith is to be without any true ground of hope for the future. It is only by faith that we have any reasonable ground for expecting any happier state of things in the new world than we have in the present.

7. To be without faith is to have no Calvary, no Saviour, no forgiveness. We only know that Jesus died for our sins, and lives again to save us from them, through believing in God. Indeed, without faith in Him life must be a dismal wilderness, and the future a dark starless blank.

II. *Not only is faith the only medium by which we can come to know and realise spiritual things, but the measure of our faith will generally be the measure of that realisation.*

In other words, the religious life of an Officer will be governed by his faith.

Salvation is commenced by means of faith, maintained by faith, and brought to a triumphant issue by faith.

1. Your conversion was by faith.

2. Your assurance of it has been received by faith.

3. Your peace and gladness have been according to your faith.

4. Your usefulness in honouring God and saving men has been, and will be, according to your faith.

5. Your triumph on your dying bed will be according to your faith.

6. Your crown, happiness, honour, and reward in Heaven will depend upon the extent to which the Spirit of Faith has led you, and enabled you to do all the holy will of God.

    (a) If you have a little faith, a half-starved, neither-hot-nor-cold affair, you will only have a little salvation.

    (b) If you have a bigger, bolder, stronger faith, you will have a bigger, grander, more glorious salvation.

    (c) If you have a full measure of faith, that is, if like Stephen and Barnabas of old, you are full of faith, and of the Holy Ghost, you will have a full measure of salvation. That is, you will have salvation up to the full limit of your capacity and need: " Good measure, pressed down, shaken together, and running over." All this is in harmony with the law laid down by Jesus Christ when He said, " According to your faith be it unto you."

Section II

The doctrine specially insisted on by the Spirit of Faith must be of great interest to Officers of The Salvation Army, because it may be truly said to govern their success.

Faith will have to do with the measure of your success; indeed, that success will be largely determined by the measure of your faith.

Other qualities and gifts will certainly be required. For instance, an Officer's success will be assisted by natural gifts and conditions; such as—

1. Good health.
2. Pleasant appearance. Beauty, comeliness, etc., will attract and impress; but here we are all at an advantage.
3. An agreeable voice.
4. Fluency in talking.
5. Intelligence.
6. Special gifts.

But all these put together will be of little service without faith. Indeed such gifts, without faith, are often a hindrance rather than a help. For, with a simple earnest faith, an Officer may do a thousand times more for God and souls without these advantages than he will do with them all, if he has no faith.

For, consider—

I. *An Officer's success will largely depend upon his faith in himself.*

1. This will apply to his personal realisation of the experience he urges on others. If he is uncertain as to whether he himself possesses the Salvation he pushes on his hearers, his trumpet cannot be expected

to do any other than give an uncertain sound. To be doubting and fearing about himself while he is talking will mean weakness and failure in all he says.

2. His success will also depend upon his faith in the consistency of his life with the standard he holds up before others.

II. *The faith of an Officer in The Army will have much to do with his success.*

It is so with me. You all know how I feel about The Army. You all know that I believe in it, and that faith helps me to study, and write, and travel, and pray, and talk, and govern. I feel that it is worth all the effort I can make. That faith cheers me in success, and comforts me in disappointments and defeat. I say to myself of a particular effort or special meeting, "If this is not as effective as I desire, it cannot prevent the onward march." For instance : If you only know and believe in The Army's history, I am sure you will fight for it. Ditto, its principles. Ditto, its system and future.

If an Officer finds himself in doubt about a Leader, or an appointment, what shall he do? Run away? No. Even if he had a General whom he did not trust, what then? Should he give up, and run away? No! *Hold on,* have faith in The Army.

III. *The measure of an Officer's faith in the comrades around him will have much to do with his success.*

If you believe in them, that faith will strengthen and comfort your heart. The thought that brave, true hearts and hands are fighting with you for the same blessed truths will be an undying stimulus. To believe that they will carry forward the work you are struggling over, when you are battling elsewhere, or when you are gone to your Heavenly Home, will be a strength to your heart. Even if there are some bad— one in so many—they were once good. But even where you have faults believe in the *good* in them. This is the principle that makes the Soldier's relations to his General so valuable. How many do your people count *you* for ?

IV. *The success of an Officer will be largely influenced by his faith in the high value of what he fights for.*

You cannot succeed without hard, self-denying, cross-bearing work. And whether you do that work heartily or not will largely depend on the estimate you set on the value of the men and women for whom you fight. If you think they are of little more value than the animals around you, you won't be very willing to suffer or sacrifice very much to save them. Who would die to save an ox or a sheep ?

A recent number of " V.C." has the following :—

" *The Lass from The Army.*"

" She was a Salvation Army lass, and her lot was a hard one. Working from seven in the morning till six o'clock at night, weaving hair-cloth, was dull and poorly-paid work, but in addition she had to bear the constant and thoughtless gibes of her fellow-workers. One autumn morning a spark from a bonfire on some adjoining allotment gardens entered an open window, alighted on a heap of loose hair, and the next minute the place was ablaze. A rush for safety of the work-girls followed. ' Is everybody down ? ' asked the foreman. His question was answered by one of the weavers, who, holding up a key, shrieked, ' My God ! I locked Lizzie Summers in the piece shed for a joke not a minute ago ! ' The piece shed was a room to be reached only through

> the burning building, through which it seemed impossible to make way. Girls and men were standing aghast and helpless, when two figures stumbled through the smoke which poured from the weaving-room. One was seen to be Lizzie Summers; the other was, for the time, unrecognisable. It was The Salvation Army lass. She had stayed behind, burnt, blistered, and half-suffocated, to batter down the door in order to liberate and save the life of her coarsest-tongued tormentor."

If you don't think that the people are of any great worth you won't be likely to face either fire or water to save them.

But if you believe—

1. That they are immortal, that they will live for ever.
2. That their souls are of indescribable worth.
3. That God loves them, and wants to get them into Heaven.
4. That Christ thought them of sufficient value to lay down His life for them.
5. That they are every hour in peril of the wrath of God and the damnation of Hell.

If you believe all this, or a reasonable part of it, you will work, and weep, and pray, and fight to save them.

Believe! Believe!

If you do not believe you will only go as far in the effort that brings success as you are forced, by custom, or orders, or salary, or the good opinion of the dying nobodies about you. If you believe a little, you will fight a little. If you believe much, you will fight much.

Richard Cecil, one of the great soul-winners of bygone days, in words which produced a great effect on my own heart, says: "Faith is the master-spring of the minister. Hell is before me and thousands of souls shut up there in everlasting agonies; Jesus Christ stands forth to save men from rushing into this bottomless abyss; He sends me to proclaim His ability and love. I want no fourth idea! Every fourth idea is contemptible! Every fourth idea is a grand impertinence!"

Faith will determine what you are and what you do.

V. *The success of an Officer will be largely influenced by his faith in the means he employs to secure that success.*

For example :—

1. *His faith in the doctrines he preaches will have to do with his success.*

If he does not really believe in them, they will have little effect on his own heart, and consequently little effect on the heart of anyone else. But if he has received them into his own soul, if they are realities to him, they will move him, and, moved by them, he will move the people he talks to. Especially if his own faith is " mixed with faith in them that hear " his message.

For instance : if he sincerely believes—

(*a*) That there is a glorious Heaven.

(*b*) That there is an awful Hell.

(*c*) That there is going to be a Judgment Day.

(*d*) That Jesus Christ came down and died for men.

(*e*) That the miseries of the people before and around him can be cleared away by the power of God, his own soul will be so moved.

2. *His faith that the truths he proclaims apply to the persons to whom he proclaims them.*

If he believes that the truth of the doctrines he preaches will take hold of the very people present at that particular time he will be likely to pour out the truth. If he is quite sure that what he has to say about conscience, and death, and Judgment, and Hell will shake the souls of the sinners who sit before him there and then, whether they be few or many, he will be likely to talk effectually, whatever the nature or size of the meeting may be.

One great reason for the marvellous power my dear wife had over the audiences she addressed was her confidence in the truth she had to preach, and in her particular manner of presenting it. "Only get them to hear me," she would say. Right or wrong, that was her notion.

3. *His faith in the methods he employs will also influence his success.*

(a) To begin with his method of working the Open-air. The Officer who does not believe in the value of the Open-air will not be likely to get much out of it. If he only regards it as a call-bird for the indoor services he will probably be content with little more than a performance. Whereas the Officer who goes for converting the people on the spot, appealing to them as they stand there, and arousing and awakening their consciences, will be likely to make his Open-air a means of great blessing to Soldiers and sinners alike. I always believed in the Open-air—hence, perhaps, my success with it.

(b) The method of conducting his indoor meetings and of carrying on all the other departments of his work, whether his visitation, his singing, his talking, his fishing, his penitent-form, or anything else. Without faith they will all be *heartless* performances —a kind of play-acting. David believed in his sling and his stones, and Goliath was as good as dead before he got at him. No doubt David's method was good, and likely to succeed, but it would have been useless to David if he had not had faith in it.

VI. *An Officer's success will be largely influenced by his faith in the actual co-operation of God with him.*

For instance, consider the effect on all he is, and says, and does, if he earnestly believes among other things:—

1. *That there is a Holy Ghost.*

I think sometimes that the practical belief in the existence of the Holy Ghost distinguishes The Army Officer from other workers around him.

2. *Again, consider the effect upon an Officer's feelings and work by a practical belief that the Spirit delights to help Officers who are striving to save and sanctify men.*

If a son was striving in a far country to know and carry out the father's law, he could rely on the father's help.

3. *Consider also that the Holy Spirit is with him while engaged in his efforts for God and souls whatever those efforts may be.*

We all know how strong and brave the company of those we love or reverence makes us in times of trial and conflict. With what courage must a firm belief in the presence and co-operation of God inspire an Officer in the fight.

VII. *It may sound strange, but there can be no question, I think, that a real faith in the actual presence and opposition of a personal Devil will help an Officer.*

It is a real *opposition.* To believe that the Devil is present and actually engaged in opposing you, will account for many things that frequently transpire in connection with an Officer's work. How you feel if the

Split Band is after a Bandsman! If the next Corps Treasurer is after a shopkeeper in your High Street for Self-Denial, though he did not give to you last year. Well, here is a roaring lion—a fiery serpent.

For instance :—

　1. Take the silly trifling of hearers that you see some-times. That can be put down to the Devil. Not always.

　2. Take the unreasonable going out of hearers. You can put that down to the Devil. Not always.

　3. Take the bad-tempered and unreasonable opposition that often has to be encountered. You can put that down to the Devil. Not always.

VIII. *An Officer's success will be very much influenced by the faith he has in results.*

It is a Spirit. They say that nothing succeeds like success. Anyway, it is difficult to secure success with-out faith.

　1. To believe in defeat is to bespeak defeat.

　2. To be afraid that nothing will happen is to make it very likely that nothing will happen.

　3. To believe that you will win is to make it very likely that you will win, and that because it will ensure the doing of your very best to secure it.

Your faith or your unbelief will influence the faith or unbelief of those about you. How eagerly the officers and soldiers watch the face of the General when a battle is going on. If they think he is confident, then they will be confident too, and fight accordingly. So that with a strong faith in victory, the battle is half-won before a blow is struck.

SECTION III

I. *I want to close this address by the mention of one aspect of the work of the Spirit of Faith which appears to me to be specially important to Salvation Army Officers.*

In point of order it ought to have been mentioned earlier on, but in view of its peculiar interest, I have reserved it to the close of my observations on the subject.

The subject to which I refer is the influence that Faith is intended to exert on an Officer's peace of mind amidst the varied and frequent trials with which he usually has to contend.

II. *I need not say that an Officer's peace of mind is intimately connected with his holiness and usefulness.*

That you all known full well, and on that ground you will know also how desirable it must be.

III. *Officers have very many trials, some of which are at times very severe.*

We all have—I am sure I have trials myself—my life has been a continued series of trials. And so it is with many of my dear Officers.

1. There are personal trials.
(*a*) Those that relate to the body.
(*b*) Those that relate to the mind.
(*c*) Those that relate to the spirit.
2. There are family trials—husband, wife, children, two sets of relatives, two mothers-in-law. If you don't want trials don't marry.
3. There are trials arising out of appointments that do not appear to fit in with our notions, and which are

often very perplexing.   Corps, Comrades, success and
failure, and many other things.

IV. *No one can claim exemption from trials.*

V. *Counsels without number of different kinds have been
propounded for dealing with trials and sorrows.*

1. The Stoical Spirit says Hide, endure.
2. The Spirit of the Coward says, When you can bear your
   sorrows no longer, run away, resign, despair, commit
   suicide.
3. The Rebellious Spirit says, Complain, murmur, turn
   infidel, kick against the pricks.   This does not answer.
4. The Worldly Spirit says, Drown your sorrows, music,
   pleasure, intoxicants, opiates.
5. Then Reason says :—

   (*a*) These things may be working out your own
   benefit.   Educating you for a higher sphere of
   honour, etc., on earth or in Heaven.

   " For our light affliction, which is but for a moment,
   worketh for us a far more exceeding and eternal
   weight of glory."

   (*b*) Reason on the subject.

   Look around and you will always find someone worse
   off than yourself.

   (*c*) The good of others—extend salvation.

   (*d*) Faith says :—

Trust in God.

   These trials are all known to God ; indeed they are all
   known to Him.   By His direct appointment, or by His
   permission.   Perhaps could not help Himself.   " It
   comes from above."

My own experience in my late trials.

   " Peace, doubting heart."

CHAPTER VIII

THE SPIRIT OF BURNING LOVE

Section I

I. *And now we come to the consideration of the message of what is, beyond question, the most attractive of the seven beautiful Spirits who are before the Throne of God, and who have occupied our attention these few days; namely, the Spirit of Love.*

His form will long linger before your eyes, and His message will tremble on your ears, for many a day. What was the message that he brought? Let me repeat it: " O Officers, Officers, commissioned by the Great ' I Am,' I come to tell you that in all you think, or speak, or do, Love must be the ruling passion of your lives." You must love each other. You must love your Soldiers. You must love poor sinners. You must love God. And that not after a fickle, cold, half-hearted fashion, but with a changeless, quenchless, Burning Love.

Now I want to remark on this message:—

1. *A widespread visitation of love is more needed by our poor undone world than all else beside.*

The vast majority of its inhabitants are hopelessly sinking down in slavery, debauchery, idolatry, and all manner of iniquities. These things lead to every kind of wretchedness in this life and in the life to come.

Luxury, law, wealth, science, learning, and no end of other human contrivances have failed to remedy this state of affairs, and will fail. Love is the remedy. Here is the Divine panacea, this is the recipe for the millennium—love. Divine love. Oh, for a deluge of this blessed spirit!

2. *My second remark is that a baptism of Divine Love is the great need of the Officers assembled at this Congress.*

I am sure that above, and beyond all else, my soul longs for a fresh and more powerful visitation of this blessed, fiery flame. In this desire I feel certain that the hunger of hundreds, nay, thousands of hearts here present, is in harmony with my own.

3. *I want to speak to you, therefore, with all the plainness and affection of which I am capable on this subject.*

I am now rapidly nearing the end of my counsels to my Field Officers. Doubtless, you think the best wine ought to come last. I think so myself, and in this subject I feel that that requirement is fully met, and it has the advantage of being equally applicable to my comrades, both on the Staff and in the Field.

4. *Divine Love is a charming theme, presenting an occasion for unending discussion, but my time will only allow me to give it a passing glance.*

For a few moments, therefore, I must ask your consideration of the effect that must inevitably follow in the heart and life of an Officer who is inspired with the all-absorbing passion of Burning Love.

II. *I need not say that the Love of which I am going to speak is the pure, unselfish affection.*

I leave out of our inquiry the human sentiment often spoken of by the term love, and which has no moral character in it. That is a mere instinct at its best, differing little from that possessed by the animal creation around us, and cannot be said to have either praise or blame attached to it. The love which would make a bear fight to the death for her cubs is on the same level with that which would make a mother die for her children. I am simply going to deal with that Holy, Celestial Flame, which, emanating from the heart of God, unselfishly seeks the highest well-being of its object, both for this world and the next.

III. *This love, like every other emotion of the human heart, can be experienced in varying degrees.*

1. There is a love that is lukewarm.

True love, beyond question, it often is, and unselfish too, but so feeble as to be scarcely worthy of the name.

2. There is a love that is fickle and spasmodic. Hot and ready to promise, to do, and to be, and suffer to-day, but cold, and powerless, and all but extinct to morrow.

3. Then there is the steady, earnest, burning passion, which, whatever feelings may come or go; whatever advantages may promise, or whatever threatenings may frown, is ever the same overpowering principle in the soul. That is what I call "Burning Love," and that is for a few minutes my theme. On it I want to say something practical and useful. How can I do so?

Oh, Thou Great God of Love, help me to speak of this, Thine adorable nature, so that I may draw out the hearts of my comrades more than ever. To wonder and admire, and to seek to have their own souls filled, absorbed, and mastered, by the celestial passion that fills, absorbs, and masters Thine.

SECTION II

Burning love in the heart, life and character of an Officer will compel him to feel, and do, and suffer many things.

I. *Among other things it will **lead** to the adoration and worship of God.*

1. By worship I mean that admiration of, and thanksgiving to the Divine Being, which ought to be realised in the hearts, and manifested in the lives, of all His intelligent creatures.

2. God ought to be worshipped. He is so great, so powerful, so good and so loving, that every being, and everything that His hand has made, ought to bless and praise Him. The Bible abounds with exhortations to worship.

3. We expect to worship Him in Heaven. To bow before His Throne, to offer Him the overflowing thanksgiving of grateful hearts, to join in the blood-washed multitude, whom no man can number, in chanting His praise, will, taken together, constitute, we anticipate, a large portion of the rapture of that Holy Place.

4. We ought to worship Him on earth.

   I think sometimes that The Salvation Army comes short in the matter of worship. I do not think that there is amongst us so much praising God for the wonders He has wrought, so much blessing Him for His every kindness, or so much adoration of His wisdom, power, and love as there might, nay, as there ought to be. You will not find too much worship in our public meetings, in our more private gatherings, or in our secret heart experiences. We do not know too much of

> " The sacred awe that dares not move,
> And all the inward Heaven of love."

Many reasons might be assigned for this if there were time. To some extent its absence can be excused. Still, it is a cause for regret. Burning love will remedy the defect. To love more will be to worship more.

5. One condition of worship is acquaintance. You must know something of the good qualities of a being before you are likely to admire and adore him. There must be a knowledge of God before the soul will prostrate itself in worship at His feet. The soul that loves God will seek His presence, delight in His communion, dwell on His perfections, and, filled with rapture by their contemplation, fall before Him and wonder and adore. Burning love will worship.

6. Gratitude is another quality essential to worship. " I thank Thee " is the first language love learns to lisp. The smallest favours bestowed by the object loved are not only noticed but magnified. Burning Love delights to bow before the Saviour and sing :—

> " Oh, let me kiss Thy bleeding feet," etc.

7. Praise is another element of worship.
The Psalmist says, " Whoso offereth praise glorifieth God." That is, makes Him more to be admired and famous in the eyes of angels and men.

Burning Love never tires of sounding forth the praises of the object loved.

(*a*) It praises Him, and His wonderful works, and all around.

(*b*) It lies before Him, and speaks them in His own listening ear.

The language of Burning Love is :—

> " I'll praise my Maker while I've breath,
> And when my voice is lost in death
>   Praise shall employ my nobler powers.
> My days of praise shall ne'er be past,
> While life, and thought, and being **last**,
>   Or immortality endures."

But worship means more than either realisation, appreciation, gratitude or praise; it means adoration.   The highest, noblest emotion of which the soul is capable. Love worships.

II. *Burning Love will promote your resemblance to God.*

As I have said, love is largely made up of admiration. What the soul admires it imitates, whether intending to do so or not.

1. This is said to be the case physically.   I have heard it said that the love existing between husbands and wives leads to their resemblance of each other in bodily appearance.

2. We see it mentally every day.

3. We know it so morally.   The company and example of good men make good men, or ought to do.   So, if you love God with this burning passion, you will, you must grow like unto Him.

III. *Burning Love promotes obedience.*

We have all heard it said that love is a slave, which means that the lover delights to do the will of the beloved. It does not have to punish itself, nor to be punished, to make it carry out the wishes of the object loved, so far as it has the ability. So, when the soul loves God, " I delight to do Thy will."

IV. *Burning Love opens to the soul new and overflowing sources of unspeakable joy.*

1. To begin with there is the joy of loving. The chief satisfaction arising from love is found not in being loved, but in loving.

2. In order to realise the true satisfaction of love, there must be love in return. A man finds no satisfaction in the love of his wife when he has ceased to love her in return, and given his affections to another woman ; in fact, then he would rather she did not love him. Her love is a torment to him, because he has ceased to love her. Just so with the love of God for us. If we do not love Him back again, we have no pleasure ; but if we give Him our hearts, we find unutterable pleasure in the love He bore to us. One cannot love a daisy or a lamb without some pleasing sensation.

3. The measure of the joy imparted by loving is proportionately increased by the greatness, and goodness, and beautifulness of the object loved. Think of loving God ! " The bliss of those who fully dwell."

V. *Burning Love will make the Officer the true friend of mankind.*

He will love men and the things of men. That is, he will unselfishly care for their well-being for their own sakes.

There is lawful and unlawful love as regards the things
of this life :—

1. The love of wrong things.

2. The wrong love of right things.

The love of God and the things of God need not lessen
an Officer's lawful love for the lawful things of earth.
It will purify and often strengthen that love, and
make it a happier love than it was before.

For, with this purified affection—

(a) He will love the things of nature.

Rivers and hills and trees and seas will now be marks
of his Father's wisdom.   He will love the lovable;
it will be his nature to do so.   His God took
pleasure in creating them.   He takes pleasure in
them to-day.   It is lawful for His children to take
pleasure in them also.

(b) With this love he will love the people about him.
His family, husband, wife, lover, friend.

(c) With this love he will love the poor, the suffering,
the weak, the hungry, the sick.   He will compassionate them.   He will go after them, and touch
them, and take them by the hand, etc.   He will
follow Jesus Christ's example, as described in the
New Testament.   Take out from it the Hospital,
the Shelter, the Food Depots, and the Rescue
Homes, and what is there left?   " Whoso hath
this world's goods, and seeth his brother have need,
and shutteth up his bowels of compassion from
him, how dwelleth the love of God in him? "

(d) With this love he will love his comrades.   In this
way they will love him back again.   Love begets
love.

VI. *Nevertheless, with all this sympathy for men and goodness, the Officer possessed of this Burning Love will be a fierce hater of evil.*

His love of God and truth and righteousness will make him the uncompromising opponent of sin. The more he loves God the more he will hate the Devil. He will not try to serve God and Mammon. The more he loves purity, the more he will hate filthiness. His love of goodness will so educate him into the understanding of the hellish character of badness, and so inflame his heart with hatred of it, that at the Last Day he will consent, nay, rejoice in the everlasting banishment from God of those who will persevere in wickedness. Love and hate are of the same burning spirit.

VII. *But, in conjunction with this hatred of evil, the Officer in whose bosom Burning Love reigns will compassionate the evil-doers.*

In the bosom of Jesus Christ there dwelt the deepest hatred of evil. And yet we read that when He beheld the multitude He had compassion on them. When, from the brow of Olivet, He beheld the men whose hearts were so mastered with evil, and so bitter in their hatred of the Son of God that they resolved to murder Him, He wept over them. When He looked down upon them in His last agony on the bloody Cross to which they had nailed Him, He prayed for their salvation, and broke His heart on their behalf.

Here is an example for us, my comrades. You and I may condemn wickedness. We must condemn it.

We cannot help but condemn and hate the drunkenness, the pride, the selfishness, the lust, and a thousand other devilish things that are carried on around us. But if we are possessed of this Burning Love we shall compassionate the guilty doers of these hateful things.

Where this Burning Love dwells in the heart of an Officer it will carry him out to look on the sinners in their homes, drink shops, haunts of vice. He will look at them as they sit before him in his Halls. His soul will go out after them. He will say of one: Think of his birth, parentage, prayerless mother, swearing father, the example of his home. Oh, my God! how I pity him! Can I help him?

Of another he will say: Oh, think of his bringing up; the school-fellows, and the filthy, lying ways they taught him almost before he knew his alphabet! Oh, my God! is the devilry we see in him to-day to be wondered at? Can I help him?

Of another he will say: Oh, remember his ignorance! How little he knows about God, and sin, and Judgment, and Heaven and Hell! And how much less he believes.

Of another he will say: Just look at his temptations, from workmates, publicans, recreations, and devils.

Of another he will say: The inconsistencies of such Christians, parsons, perhaps Salvationists, as he has met with, they have blighted him.

Of another he will say: Oh, remember his failures! How often he has tried. They have given up counting the times he has been to the penitent-form. Weeping at the mercy-seat one night; mocking with his mates, or rolling drunk to his home the next.

Poor wretch! O God! how I pity him. What can I do to help him?

Of another : Think of his misery, his wretched health, his comfortless home.

Of yet another : Think of his cantankerous nature, his natural "cussedness," his rebellious or wobbling nature and feeble will. Again, think of that man's coming doom. He will be in Hell soon! And then there will come the reflection : "What might I not have been had I been circumstanced and tempted as these poor sinners and backsliders have been!" As John Bradford said when he saw a criminal being led to execution : "But for the grace of God, there goes John Bradford."

VIII. *This Burning Love will make the Officer in whose bosom it dwells not only compassionate, but willing to suffer on behalf of the evil-doers.*

A willingness to suffer on behalf of those whom you love is inseparable from all true affection.

You will find plenty of examples of this even among the creatures whose love is really only instinct, as it is in the animal creation.

You will find more in man with his ordinary instinct.

   (*a*) What wonderful things a mother's love will make her do and suffer! No hardship is counted too great.

   (*b*) What marvels the love of the patriot will accomplish!

How willingly, eagerly, the love of country has carried them to deeds of daring, suffering, and death. How the Japs have gone singing and triumphantly shouting to certain destruction. Consecration signed in blood! But this love is better than the love of kindred, and country, and friends, which has ordinarily some selfish interest behind it.

Burning Love unselfishly suffers for its own enemies, and for those whom it knows to be the foes of God and man.

(i.) It was this Burning Love that carried the prophets of old through hardships and suffering and death. Read the history of Moses and the account of God's heroes in the Epistle to the Hebrews.

(ii.) It was this Burning Love that carried Jesus Christ to the Cross.

(iii.) It was this Burning Love that carried the Apostles and martyrs on to their end.

(iv.) It was this Burning Love that carried millions and millions more since that day to a triumphant finish.

(v.) This Burning Love will make Officers preach, pray, visit, deal with difficulties in their Corps, and go to the end of the earth to save souls.

IX. *Burning Love will make the Officer the beloved of—*

1. Comrades. How Officers complain about their comrades. Some are not loved. Why? Is it not because the Officer has not sufficiently loved them?

2. Those for whom he fights. The weak, the afflicted, the children.

3. God and the angels. Ministering spirits will attend him in his labours.

X. *Burning Love will ensure the Officer's perseverance.* While this love burns, no fear of retreat.

XI. *Burning Love will crown the Officer with glory in the world to come.*

Celestial rewards will not be according to—

1. Gifts, talents, brilliance of intellect, etc.
2. The number and magnitude of the miracles wrought on the earth.
3. The number of souls won.
4. But according to the measure of love. " She loved much." " Love never faileth : but whether there be prophecies, they shall fail; whether there be tongues, they shall cease; whether there be knowledge, it shall vanish away. . . . And now abideth faith, hope, love, these three; but the greatest of these is love."

That is the standard by which God measures the value of your service on earth, and by which He will measure your reward in Heaven.

XII. *Burning Love, the most precious of all gifts, is within the reach of all.*

The human gifts counted of most value by men are denied to many. All cannot excel in the gift of praying or talking. But all can have the Spirit of Burning Love.

SOME BOOKS BY OR ABOUT
WILLIAM and CATHERINE BOOTH

Mrs. Booth by W.T. Stead

General Booth by W.T. Stead

Catherine Booth by Catherine Bramwell Booth

In Darkest England and The Way Out
  by William Booth

Female Ministry by Catherine Booth

The Founder Speaks Again by William Booth

The General Next to God by Richard Collier

How to Preach by William Booth

A Ladder to Holiness—Tract by William Booth

A Ladder to Salvation—Tract by William Booth

Salvation Soldiery by William Booth

The Seven Spirits or What I Teach My Officers
  by William Booth

Sergeant Major Do Your Best by William Booth

The Story of Catherine Booth for Young People
  by Mildred Duff

They Said It by William and Catherine Booth

William Booth Speaks to Youth—Tract
  by William Booth

Words of Catherine Booth

Words of William Booth